THE WOMEN
OF THE
MAYFLOWER

A COLLECTION OF
EXCERPTS REMEMBERING THE
WOMEN THAT HISTORY FORGOT

By

VARIOUS

Read & Co.

Copyright © 2020 Read & Co. History

This edition is published by Read & Co. History,
an imprint of Read & Co.

This book is copyright and may not be reproduced or copied in any
way without the express permission of the publisher in writing.

British Library Cataloguing-in-Publication Data
A catalogue record for this book is available
from the British Library.

Read & Co. is part of Read Books Ltd.
For more information visit
www.readandcobooks.co.uk

CONTENTS

WOMEN PIONEERS
By Mrs. John A. Logan 7

MATRONS AND MAIDENS
WHO CAME IN THE MAYFLOWER
By Annie Russell Marble 97

AN EXCERPT OF LETTER X
By Fredrika Bremer 117

"The Pilgrim's wild and wintry day
Its shadow round us draws;
The Mayflower of his stormy bay,
Our Freedom's struggling cause."

"But warmer suns erelong shall bring
To life the frozen sod;
And, through dead leaves of hope, shall spring
Afresh the flowers of Cod!"

—JOHN GREENLEAF WHITTIER,
The Mayflowers, 1856

WOMEN PIONEERS

By Mrs. John A. Logan

The Guiding Hand of Deity, as in all things, can be seen in the ultimate landing of the Pilgrims at Plymouth, New England. The persecutions inflicted by the bishops and zealots upon dissenters from the mother church, who were denominated "Separatists" caused them to seek a new field where they hoped to be allowed to worship God according to the dictates of their own consciences.

After many unsuccessful attempts, they finally left England, in 1608, and took up their abode in Amsterdam, Holland. There are many conflicting traditions and reports as to the welcome they received in Dutchland. There was, beyond question, disinclination on the part of the Ruler and the people to extend to them cordial hospitality, lest the friendly relations might be interrupted between England and Holland. They were, however, allowed to remain at Amsterdam until, of their own volition, they removed to Leyden, the principal manufacturing town of the Netherlands. They hoped by this change to better their condition and secure employment for the artisans among them who had had training and experience in the factories in England. They endured unspeakable hardships, disappointments and the loss of many of their numbers in Holland. They had gained little but respite from persecution by leaving their homes in England.

Their saintly Bishop, John Robinson by name, hoped that at Leyden, with more lucrative resources, through the possibility of securing employment, they might eventually obtain permanent homes and probably increase the number of followers of their

7

creed. They soon found, however, that Leyden offered little encouragement.

Meanwhile, they heard marvelous stories of the American Continent and of the opportunities it offered for material prosperity, absolute freedom of conscience and perfect religious liberty.

It had been impossible, handicapped as they were by untoward environment, for them to save any money or extend their privileges in any manner. Chained by necessity to daily arduous labor for existence, and enfeebled by illness and misfortunes, they were well nigh exhausted when relief came in the form of agents seeking colonists for America, and "Merchant Adventurers" trying to procure settlers for rich plantations in the new country. The povery of these noble people is evident from the hard terms to which they were obliged to submit in their contracts with the agents and the "Merchant Adventurers" to procure passage to the Land of Hope and Liberty.

After months of negotiations, the Pilgrims finally embarked on the Speedwell, a craft scarcely sea-worthy for the voyage from Delfshaven to Southampton to join the proposed expedition. They reached that port after perilous experiences, which had the effect of discouraging very many of the party, causing the dispirited to abandon their leaders on their arrival at Southampton.

However, the indomitable spirits of such men as Robert Cushman, John Carver, and others were not to be dissuaded from their purpose. Hence, after another long period of waiting and tedious negotiations with the "Merchant Adventurers" and agents of companies interested in securing colonists for the New World, the Mayflower was chartered between the 12th and 22nd of June, 1620. Captain Thomas Jones was in command of the ship; John Clarke as first mate or pilot, an experienced navigator, having crossed the Atlantic many times previously; Robert Coppin was second mate or pilot—he had been once at least on a voyage to the New World; Master Williamson, purser;

Dr. Giles Heale, from discovery by the Mayflower descendants, was, doubtless, surgeon of the Mayflower.

There were on board one hundred and two souls. The ship was poorly provided with means of defense, having but three pieces of ordnance and some small arms and ammunition. But these brave souls, some of them with families, and their meagre household effects, dared to set out for a land where they hoped to secure not only religious liberty but opportunity for amassing fortunes.

Alack! with all their religious fervor and heroism "a man's a man for a' that," and it required skilful management on the part of the wisest to adjust the many difficulties and dissolve the innumerable conspiracies that were continually being formed between the zealous but unreasonable religionists and the agents of the "Merchant Adventurers" to change the plans of the leaders of the sect, whose chief object was to establish a colony of their own faith.

Floating the English Union Jack, the Mayflower was piloted by Thomas English, the helmsman of the shallop of the Mayflower, into Plymouth harbor and safely anchored on the stormy night of Sunday, December 16, 1620, thus ending the long voyage of the Pilgrims from Plymouth, England, to Plymouth, New England, in one hundred and fifty-five days. Looking back across the centuries that have intervened, it would be difficult to imagine the emotions that swelled the hearts of those devout people as they stepped upon the soil of the promised land upon which they had builded so many bright hopes. From the Log of the Mayflower, given by Dr. Azel Ames, we learn that there disembarked from the Mayflower one hundred and three souls on that bleak Sunday, December 16, 1620,—seventy-five men and boys and twenty-eight women and girls. Sad to relate, one-half of that number were laid "beneath the sod of their new home before it was clothed by the Spring's verdure."

History and tradition have made heroes of many of the men, and they were entitled to far more glory than they have ever received for their heroic daring. Alas! of the women who shared the burdens and displayed equal courage with the men, little to their credit has been preserved by tradition or history. But when one recalls that in those days women had not the privileges they have now, one realizes that their self-denial, heroism, patience and long-suffering were accepted as a matter of course and no note was taken of it by their selfish liege lords.

In the enlightenment of the twentieth century, one recognizes that the women were the martyrs of that long and perilous voyage. It was the women who kept the weary vigils through sunshine and storm; it was the wives and mothers who were the nurses and comforters of their families; they cooked and cleaned and helped to keep the Mayflower habitable. There were, doubtless, times when weaker women would have been a burden to the men, who had hourly difficulties to overcome, which taxed their courage and strength almost to the point of exhaustion.

When at last they landed, they received a cold reception, not only on account of the inclemency of the midwinter weather, but because the natives were far from cordial in their greetings to strangers whom they suspected had designs upon what they considered their country. They had watched the inroads upon their domain and invasion of their rights by those who had preceded the Pilgrims, and regarded this new intrusion as boding ill for them. However, these brave people set to work religiously to win their way to the confidence and toleration of the savages to whose country they had fled for liberty.

History has long since told the story of the Puritan victories under the banner of the Cross, and of the constant additions to their numbers as soon as the news of the successful landing of the expedition and their auspicious prospects was wafted across the seas to the Old World. At the time, they did not fully appreciate the limitless scope of the blessings their labors, endurance and wisdom under the guidance of the Infinite would bring to the unborn millions of human souls of all land who have continually, to this day, sought freedom of thought, personal rights, and religious liberty in our great American Republic, whose foundation was laid by the Pilgrims who came to our shores in the Mayflower.

It has long since been admitted that mothers have always had all to do with the instilling of principles and developing the character of children. Upon this hypothesis, it is easy to account for the sterling qualities which have characterized New England men and women and given them the leadership in the early days of the Republic in religious education and patriotism. Their Puritan mothers, with their deep religious convictions and conscientious scruples as to the discharge of every duty of life, instilled in their offspring their own exalted religious principles. These sons and daughters, as time has rolled on, have followed the course of the Empire and set up altars to Almighty God and their Country wherever they have halted to establish homes.

As civilization has step by step pushed forward its boundaries from the Atlantic to the Pacific, the same principles of religion and patriotism have inspired the succeeding generations until the American Republic represents the full fruition of the tree of liberty planted so firmly on Plymouth Rock by the Pilgrims.

Unless one has attempted a research of the records, they cannot possibly realize how little has been written of the achievements of the women of the American Nation, notwithstanding the fact that since the landing of the Pilgrims women have stood side by side with the men in the marvelous development of the resources of the New World and the advancement of modern civilization.

The correct explanation of this curious phenomenon lies in the indisputable truth that the brave women who embarked on the Mayflower as the wives and daughters of the adventurous Pilgrims had always been subservient to the male members of their families. The Pilgrim Fathers, laboring under the influence of fanaticism, believed that the Old and New Testaments placed women under the domination of men. Acting upon this conviction, they appropriated the fruits of their women

11

companions' self-sacrifice, intuitive knowledge, inventive genius, wise suggestions and natural diplomacy as their very own, without giving the women any credit whatever or making any note or acknowledgment of the influence and aid of the women who shared in all of the trials and hardships of the perilous voyage across the seas and in establishing homes in the wilderness of the New World.

The examples of the Pilgrim Fathers were followed by their sons for generations. The men, in keeping the records and in 'handing down the traditions, naturally neglected to "render unto Cæsar that which was Cæsar's." The few women shared nobly in the indescribable hardships and suffering experienced by the indomitable spirits who made the first settlements on the shores of New England. Neither history nor tradition has accorded to these women the meed of praise so justly their due. It is left to one's imagination to picture their patience, forbearance, fortitude, quick perception, dauntless courage and intelligence in discharging the duties that fell upon these women as wives, mothers, nurses and companions of men imbued with the idea of their superiority and whose selfishness was prodigious. Trained in the rough school of pioneer struggles which required physical strength, brute force, daring courage, and contempt for weakness, one can readily understand that they were unmindful of the finer feelings and tenderness which are the natural fruits of civilization, and that the men accepted the help of the women as their legitimate rights.

When at last an era of success dawned, it was natural that the men as the leaders of the adventurous settlers of the New World should have all the glory and that the prodigious labors and sacrifices of the women should be overlooked. Half a century had passed before women were accorded any measure of their deserts. During the two-thirds of a century since women had any recognition, they have step by step won their way to equality in all respects, save perhaps physically, to the men, though the privilege of suffrage and representation is not accorded in every state because the women themselves disagree upon the expediency of being given the right of suffrage. With this exception, every avenue is open to women in this "land of the free and the home of the brave."

So well and intelligently have women improved their opportunities that to them belongs the credit of greatly expediting the progress of Christianity, education, and civilization. The natural intuitions of women in the discovery of the good in all things and their keen perception as to how to develop that good are admitted. Julia Ward Howe wrote in the preface of a book "Woman is primarily the mother of the human race. She is man's earliest and tenderest guardian, his life-long companion, his trusted adviser and friend. Her breath is the music of the nursery; the incense of the church." Woman's mission and sphere is thus graphically portrayed by the gifted pen of one of the noblest women of our race.

The majority of women have exemplified this aphorism by the faithful performance of their duties as wives, mothers and members of society. In three or four decades they have succeeded in demonstrating their abilities in fields other than domestic drudgery to which they were assigned in the earlier days of the Republic through the misconception of Bible truths, fanaticism and the prejudices of the unenlightened. The barriers erected by the Puritans have been broken down and women during the last half century in almost equal numbers with men have contested successfully for the honors in science, literature, music, art, political economy, education, the professions of law, medicine and theology, and also in many of the vocations of life which are based on industrial principles—to say nothing of her achievements in the higher realms of Christianity, humanity, philanthropy and in the solution of the problems of social purity, domestic science, municipal administration, cultivation and betterment of the conditions of mankind.

The majority of women as "mothers of the race" have the advantage in that they have the power to transmit to their offspring principles which inspire high ambitions, noble instincts, pure thoughts and inclination for right living. They have in their keeping the infant minds which they can mould and train for noble or ignoble lives. Unfortunately, the influence of mothers does not invariably abide in their children, but in most cases it is felt from the cradle to the grave by the children they have borne and reared properly.

THE EARLY PERIOD OF SETTLEMENT

Jamestown was founded May 13, 1607, and the first woman of whom we have any mention in that settlement was Mistress Forest and her maid, Ann Burrs, and she is supposed to have been the first English woman married on American soil. The terrible sufferings of these settlers from starvation and want is a matter of history, and not more than sixty of the original five hundred souls remained after what is known as the "Starving Time," and it is a most remarkable fact that of these sixty survivors a large proportion were women. In 1621 it became evident that a new lot of settlers must be brought out to America if this new colony was to survive. Sir Edwin Sandys, at the head of the London Company, who had charge of the interests of the Virginia settlers, adopted the plan of sending out wives, respectable young women, to these planters, and in one year he sent over one thousand two hundred and sixty-one new settlers, and on one voyage ninety women were sent to become the wives of these hardy pioneers. Being of a thrifty turn this English company did not do this from a purely disinterested motive, as they required pay from each man who thus secured a wife, and the price fixed was one hundred and twenty pounds of tobacco, about eighty dollars of our present money. The contract, however, was permitted to be a free one on the part of the woman, and she could not be forced into contracting a marriage objectionable to her, but history tells us that no maiden remained unmarried out of this first venture.

In November, 1620, the Pilgrim fathers landed from "The Mayflower" at Plymouth Rock, Massachusetts, and Mary Chilton, it is said, was the first to place her foot upon American soil. The day after the arrival of these Pilgrims, the first child was born. The parents were William and Susanna White. The son was named Peregrine, which signifies Pilgrim. There are very few records of any women of conspicuous effort or influence at this time. Longfellow's poem, "The Courtship of Miles Standish" is familiar to us all and presents a more or less authentic picture of the lives of the women of that day in New England.

The wives of the Pilgrims were: Mrs. Katherine Carver, Mrs. Dorothy Bidford, Mrs. Elizabeth Winslow, Mrs. Mary Brewster, Mrs. Mary Allerton, Mrs. Elizabeth Hopkins, the two Mrs. Tilley, Mrs. Tinker, Mrs. Rigdale, Mrs. Rose Standish, Mrs. Martin, Mrs. Mullens, Mrs. Susanna White, Mrs. Sarah Eaton, Mrs. Chilton, Mrs. Fuller, and Mrs. Helen Billington. The daughters of these Pilgrim mothers were: Elizabeth Tilley, Remember Allerton, Mary Allerton, Constance Hopkins, Damaris Hopkins, Mary Chilton, and Priscilla Mullens, and Desire Minter may be listed as a "Mayflower" daughter. "Mrs. Carver's maid" must also be mentioned among the women of the Mayflower, and even the little "bound" girl, Ellen More, is worthy of place in this distinguished group.

KATHERINE CARVER

Mrs. Katherine Carver, it has been supposed by some, was a sister of Pastor Robinson. This supposition rests, apparently, upon the expression in his parting letter to Carver, where he says: "What shall I say unto you and your good wife, my loving sister?" Neither the place of Mrs. Carver's nativity nor her age is known.

DESIRE MINTER

Desire Minter was evidently a young girl of the Leyden congregation, between the ages of fourteen and seventeen, who, in some way (perhaps through kinship), had been taken into Carver's family. She returned to England early.

"MRS. CARVER'S MAID.

"Mrs. Carver's maid," it is fair to presume, from her position as lady's maid and its requirements in those days, was a young woman of eighteen or twenty years, and this is confirmed by her early marriage. Nothing is known of her before the embarkation. She died early.

MARY BREWSTER

The wife of Elder Brewster, the "Chief of the Pilgrims," was about fifty-one years of age at the time of the landing of the Mayflower. She was the mother of three sons; the two younger, Love and Wrestling Brewster, accompanied their parents to the new land.

ELIZABETH (BARKER) WINSLOW

Mrs. Elizabeth (Barker) Winslow, the first wife of the Governor, appears by the data supplied by the record of her marriage in Holland, May 27, 1618, to have been a maiden of comporting years to her husband's, he being then twenty-three. Tradition makes her slightly younger than her husband.

ELLEN MORE

Ellen More, "a little girl that was put to him" (Winslow), died early. She was a sister of the other More children, "bound out" to Carver and Brewster.

MRS. DOROTHY (MAY) BRADFORD

Mrs. Dorothy (May) Bradford's age (the first wife of the Governor) is fixed at twenty-three by collateral data, but she may have been older. She was probably from Wisbeach, England. The manner of her tragic death (by drowning, having fallen overboard from the ship in Cape Cod harbor), the first violent death in the colony, was especially sad, her husband being absent for a week afterward. It is not known that her body was recovered.

MARY (NORRIS) ALLERTON

Mary (Norris) Allerton is called a "maid of Newberry in England," in the Leyden record of her marriage, in October, 1611, and it is the only hint as to her age we have. She was presumably a young woman. Her death followed (a month later) the birth of her still-born son, on board the Mayflower in Plymouth Harbor, February 25, 1621.

REMEMBER ALLERTON

Remember Allerton, apparently Allerton's second child, was, no doubt, born in Holland about 1614. She married Moses Maverick by 1635. and Thomas Weston's only child, Elizabeth, was married from her house at Marblehead. to Roger Conant, the first "governor" of a "plantation" on the Massachusetts Bay territory.

MARY ALLERTON

Mary Allerton, apparently the third child, could hardly have been much more than four years old in 1620. She was probably born in Holland about 1616. She was the last survivor of the passengers of the Mayflower, dying at Plymouth, New England, 1699.

SUSANNA (FULLER) WHITE

Susanna (Fuller) White, wife of William, and sister of Dr. Fuller (?), was apparently somewhat younger than her first husband and perhaps older than her second. She must, in all probability (having been married in Leyden in 1612), have been at least twenty-five at the embarkation eight years later. Her second husband, Governor Winslow, was but twenty-five in 1620, and the presumption is that she was slightly his senior. There appears no good reason for ascribing to her the austere and rather unlovable characteristics which the pen of Mrs. Austin has given her.

ALICE MULLENS

Mrs. Alice Mullens, whose given name we know only from her husband's will, filed in London, we know little about. Her age was (if she was his first wife) presumably about that of her husband, whom she survived but a short time.

PRISCILLA MULLENS

Priscilla Mullens, whom the glamour of unfounded romance and the pen of the poet Longfellow have made one of the best known and best beloved of the Pilgrim band, was either a little older or younger than her brother Joseph—it is not certain which. But that she was over sixteen is probable.

ELIZABETH HOPKINS

Nothing is known concerning Mrs. Elizabeth Hopkins, except that she was not her husband's first wife. Some time apparently elapsed between her husband's marriages.

CONSTANCE (OR CONSTANTIA) HOPKINS

Constance (or Constantia) Hopkins was apparently about eleven years old in 1620, as she married in 1627, and probably was then not far from eighteen years old.

DAMARIS HOPKINS

Damaris Hopkins, the younger daughter of Master Hopkins, was probably a very young child when she came in the Mayflower, but her exact age has not been ascertained. Davis, as elsewhere noted, makes the singular mistake of saying she was born after her parents arrived in New England. She married Jacob Cooke, and the ante-nuptial agreement of his parents is believed to be the earliest of record in America, except that between Gregory Armstrong and the widow Billington.

HUMILITY COOPER

Humility Cooper is said by Bradford to have been a "cosen" of the Tilleys, but no light is given as to her age or antecedents. She was but a child apparently. She returned to England very soon after the death of Mr. and Mrs. Tilley, and "died young."

BRIDGET (VAN DER VELDE) TILLEY

Mrs. Bridget (Van der Velde) Tilley was her husband's second wife, concerning whom nothing is known, except that she was of Holland, and that she had, apparently, no child.

ELIZABETH TILLEY

Elizabeth Tilley is said, by Goodwin and others, to have been fourteen years old at her parents' death in 1621, soon after the arrival in New England. She was the child of her father's first wife. She married John Howland before 1624. Historians for many years called her the "daughter of Governor Carver," but the recovery of Bradford's MS. "historie" corrected this, with many other misconceptions, though to some the error had become apparent before.

MRS. CHILTON

Mrs. Chilton's given name is declared by one writer to have been Susanna, but it is not clearly proven. Whence she came, her ancestry, and her age, are alike unknown.

MARY CHILTON

Mary Chilton was but a young girl in 1620. She married, before 1627, John Winslow, and was probably not over fourteen when she came with her parents in the Mayflower.

SARAH EATON

Mrs. Sarah Eaton, wife of Francis, was evidently a young woman, with an infant, at the date of embarkation. Nothing more is known of her, except that she died in the spring following the arrival at Plymouth.

ELLEN (OR "ELEN") BILLINGTON

Mrs. Ellen (or "Elen") Billington, as Bradford spells the name, was evidently of comporting age to her husband's, perhaps a little younger. Their two sons, John and Francis, were lively urchins who frequently made matters interesting for the colonists, afloat and ashore. The family was radically bad throughout, but they have had not a few worthy descendants. Mrs. Billington married Gregory Armstrong, and their ante-nuptial agreement is the first such record known in America.

One of the most powerful influences exercised by the women pioneers was the influence for religion. Every pioneer woman was transfused with a deep, glowing, unwavering religious faith, and through all the terrible trials of those earliest days, as well as through those of the generations which followed, their faith never wavered, and at all times proved a bulwark of strength in seasons of trouble.

In 1630, we find the name of Lady Arabella Johnson, wife of Isaac Johnson, among those who came with the fleet of eleven ships to Massachusetts Bay, driven out of England by the religious persecution of the time. In this same colony of Pilgrims came one, Ann Dudley, the daughter of an old servant of the Count of Lincoln, father of Lady Arabella Johnson, and married to one Simon Bradstreet, who afterward became Governor of Massachusetts. She was a Puritan of the strictest Puritan type. She became quite famous as a poetess, and there were but few writers of that day. Governor Winthrop's wife was one of the early authors and when she lost her mind it was claimed by her Puritanical feminine friends that this was caused by her deserting her domestic duties and meddling with such things as were proper only for men.

Some idea of the severity of those days can be gained through the fact that in 1634, there was enacted a law which forbade any person, either man or woman, to make or buy any "woolen, silk, or linen with any lace on it, silver or gold thread, under the penalty of forfeiture of said clothes. Gold and silver girdles, hat bands, belts, ruffs, and beaver hats were prohibited, the planters being permitted to wear out such apparel as they were already provided with." Five years later another law prohibited "immoderate great breeches, knots of ryban, broad shoulder bands, and rayles, silk ruses, double ruffles and capes," and should any person wear such apparel they were fined ten shillings, or any tailor make a garment of these materials he was fined ten shillings. Notwithstanding the strict ideas of those days the story is told of one Agnes Surriage, a servant and mere drudge, scrubbing the floor of the tavern at Marblehead, attracting the attention of young Sir Harry Frankland, collector of the Port of Boston. He became so infatuated with her beauty that he had her educated by the best masters in Boston and instructed in religion by Dr. Edward Holyoke, president of Harvard College, but did not honor her with his name until the terrors of the earthquake in 1755, in Lisbon, brought him to a realization of her position, and they were married. She became Lady Frankland and was later received with great honor in England. He was appointed Consul-General at Lisbon, but died in 1768, in England, and Lady Frankland returned to America. During the Revolution she suffered exile as a Tory. She later married John Drew, a rich banker, and died at the age of fifty-eight, having been one of the most prominent figures in Colonial history.

In 1689, Mr. Paris came to Salem from the West Indies, bringing with him two colored servants, John an Indian, and Tituba his wife. Like all people of their race, they were full of superstitious belief in second sight, and so infected the village of Salem that many young girls were brought under their influence and learned to go into trances and prate all manner of foolishness. This brought about the belief that they were possessed of witches. Chief among these young people were Mary Walker, Mary Hubbard, Elizabeth Booth, Susan Sheldon, Mary Warren, and Sarah Churchill, young girls still in their teens, with Ann Putnam and Mary Lewis, the latter two being most prominent. Mrs. Ann Putnam, about thirty years of age, and, it is supposed now, of unsound mind, was a beautiful and well-educated woman. She became the leader in this mischief. Tituba, the Indian hag, had associated with her two old women by the name of Sarah Good and Sarah Osborne. They were finally brought to Boston for trial and they implicated two respectable women of the community, Martha Corey and Rebecca Nurse. This mania became almost an epidemic. Men were even accused and the best women were not saved from the accusations of this evil-minded coterie. Susan Martin was accused on the ground that she walked on a country road without getting her skirts and feet muddy and must be a witch. A special court finally had to be appointed by Sir William Phipps, the first Governor, to try these women, when nineteen suffered death. Charges were even brought against Lady Phipps, the wife of the Governor. The death blow to this panic was given when some people of Andover on being accused brought suit for defamation of character in the courts.

ANNE HUTCHINSON

When the ship "Griffin" arrived in the port of Boston, on the 18th day of September, 1634, that band of Puritan settlers who set forth from the embryo town to meet and welcome the newcomers would have been very much disturbed and astonished if they had known that there was one among that ship's company who was to bring great trouble to the feeble Colony and still greater calamity upon herself. Anne Hutchinson was to play the most conspicuous part in a great religious controversy; it was something more vital than a mere theological dispute; it was the first of many New England quickenings in the direction of social, intellectual and political development; in fact New England's earliest protest against formulas. Its leader was a woman whose name should be written large as one of the very few women who have really influenced the course of events in American history. It is indeed curious that at that time, when women held such an inferior position in the intellectual world, heads of councils of state and hoary-headed ministers should have allowed themselves to be involved in controversy in which their chief adversary was a woman.

Anne Hutchinson was born at Alford, in Lincolnshire, not far from Boston, England, on the 28th of July, 1591, so that she must have been forty-three years old when she came to Boston, though her comely figure and attractive face and engaging manners gave her a much more youthful appearance. Her father was a college man and her mother was a great-aunt of the poet Dryden, and was also related to the family from which descended the famous writer, Jonathan Swift, so Anne from both parents inherited intellect and force. Her marriage with William Hutchinson was the result of pure and disinterested love, for he had no right to heraldic devices. Of this husband little need be said. He is described by contemporaries as a man of very mild temper and weak parts, and wholly guided by his wife. Perhaps this was fortunate, considering his wife's strong and dominant will.

Things might have gone well for Mistress Hutchinson in the Colony had she not fallen into some heated disputes on certain religious subjects with one of her fellow-voyagers on board the "Griffin." This resulted in her adversary's, the Rev. Zechariah Symmes, gaining a deep and bitter animosity toward her. No sooner had they landed than he took occasion to denounce her as a prophetess—a dangerous accusation in those days. Regardless of her "Reverend" foe she immediately began to teach her new strange doctrines to those about her. And almost all of Puritan Boston fell under the spell of her eloquence and her magnetic charm. The women crowded her home to hear her read from the Scriptures and explain texts, and, it must be admitted, criticised the preachers, for this powerful woman was not afraid to express her opinion with dangerous candor. Boston was really at that period under a religious despotism. Looking back upon those times, it seems strange that the early Puritan settlers, beset as they were with bodily danger and physical hardship, should have spent so much of their time in splitting hairs upon theological subjects. It was, nevertheless, significant of an intellectual unrest, which was to result in people doing their own thinking. This has always been a marked characteristic of the American—one of which we are justly particular, and it should be remembered that this young woman was its pioneer. Mistress Anne Hutchinson taught that the Gospel of Christ had superseded the law of Moses that no matter what sin overtook one who had received the gift of the "Crest of Love," he was still one of the elect; that the spirit of the Holy Ghost dwells in a "Justified Person," and other things that nobody understands and nobody is foolish enough to bother about in these days. In 1634, Mistress Hutchinson and her followers and the ministers of the Boston Church wrangled over these confusing and unnecessary doctrines until it is very likely they themselves became very much mixed up. It is what historians call the Antinomian Controversy. Antinomy being opposed to the law, Winthrop and Endicott considered it a very dangerous heresy. Mistress Anne was finally brought to trial for her teachings—a thing she could hardly have failed to expect, for though she was a gentle and patient nurse to the sick, a fond wife and mother, and a Godly woman, still she was transgressing her right in openly setting up a new creed among, the people with whom she had chosen to dwell. Among the ministers there were two of whom she earnestly approved, the Rev. Mr. Cotton and Joseph Wheelwright, her brother-in-law. But the preachings and teachings of all the others she earnestly condemned, which made these narrow-minded spiritual ministers her mortal enemies. In 1637, the Rev. John Cotton, who had appeared to share Anne Hutchinson's opinions to some extent, changed his course and the way was prepared for her accusation and trial. This trial was before the Court of Magistrates, at Cambridge, November, 1637, and to quote from Jared Sparks, "It will be allowed by most readers to have been one of the most shameful proceedings recorded in the annals of Protestantism." The scene must have been an impressive one—the dignified Governor Winthrop, grave, strong, courteous, but already convinced of the culprit's guilt; Endicott, who, as Hawthorne says, "Would stand with his drawn sword at the Gate of Heaven and resist to the death all pilgrims thither except they traveled his own path"; Bradstreet, Nowell, Stoughton, Welde, all her judges and her enemies. As the biting north wind swept cold gusts through the bare room in which the assemblage sat on that November day, the defenseless woman must have felt that the cold gale that blew from the gloomy wilderness on the desolate shore was no more chilling than the hearts of her judges. She was ill and faint, but she was allowed neither food nor a seat during that long exhausting day, until she fell to the floor from weakness, while first one and then another of them plied her with questions. And, as Anne Hutchinson answered these questions clearly and sensibly, quoting passages from the Scriptures to prove that she had done nothing unlawful, nothing worthy of condemnation, perhaps she may have felt, even among her enemies and with no hand stretched out toward her, a thrill of pride in her heart that she, a woman without the influence of wealth or station, was pitting her intellect against that of the wisest men in the Colony. No matter what the issue should be the fact of her trial was an acknowledgment of her power and influence—a power and influence never before nor since equaled in this country.

Of an intensely spiritual nature and of rare elevation of purpose, Anne Hutchinson stood that day for the principle of liberty of speech, and the seed planted almost three hundred years ago has grown into the glorious religious and intellectual freedom of to-day.

At the conclusion of the trial, when she heard the verdict of banishment, Anne Hutchinson, turning to Winthrop said boldly, "I desire to know wherefore I am banished." He replied, with high-handed superciliousness, "Say no more, the court knows wherefore and is satisfied."

Joseph Welde was the brother of Rev. Thomas Welde, who had been her bitterest enemy, and he had called her the "American Jezebel," so she had little to expect in the way of consideration and comfort. But the banished woman had followers and the court found it expedient to issue an order that "All those whose names are under written shall upon warning give all such guns, pistols, swords, pewter shot and matches over to their custody upon penalty of 10 pounds." This shows that the magistrates feared violence from those who believed in Mistress Hutchinson and loved and revered their teacher.

Having been excommunicated from the Boston Church, and admonished for her grievous sins she was ordered to leave Massachusetts by the end of March. And on the twenty-eighth of that month Anne Hutchinson set forth upon her journey to Aquidneck, R. L, where she hoped to commune with God and her fellow-beings according to the dictates of her conscience. Many Bostonians followed her and amid the forests of Rhode Island she found for a little while a peaceful life. But even here she was not spared from her old persecutors, who still feared that a new sect might arise in their neighborhood. Mrs. Hutchinson, whose husband had died, determined to go into the Dutch Colony of the New Netherlands where the magistrates did not care quite so much what the colonists believed, and eventually she planned her settlement in the solitude of what is now called Rochelle. A swamp in the vicinity of her cottage still bears the name of Hutchinson's river and we may imagine how as the evening shades closed in upon them the settlers would gather around their leader, who read from the Scriptures and exhorted them to continue steadfast in the faith she had delivered to them. As the candle-lights shone and flickered on her strong face with its lines of struggle and of sorrow and was reflected in the deep, dark eyes, she seemed a woman who had fled away to this remote spot divinely inspired.

But she had chosen a bad time to come to this part of the country, for while safe from the men of her own race, who had given her nothing but injustice and persecution, she was surrounded by dangers from the natives. Governor Kieft, the Dutch Governor, had by cruel treatment aroused the Indians to sullen resentment. Not long after the arrival of Anne Hutchinson and her little colony, savage hostilities broke out. Suddenly, when the New Netherlander were unprepared, an army of fifteen hundred swarthy warriors swept over Long Island, killing, burning and torturing the settlers on Manhattan Island and carrying their savage warfare to the very gates of the fort.

Far out across the Harlem River, Anne Hutchinson's weak settlement of sixteen souls was at the mercy of the merciless Indians. The chief who had entered the land of this section according to tribal laws had sent to find out the strength and weakness of the colony. The messenger was treated with the hospitality which it was a part of Anne Hutchinson's religion to show to the "Stranger" who came within her gates. But the Indian spy was the messenger of death, for that night the colony was attacked and every one of that little settlement perished by clubs or tomahawks. Anne Hutchinson and her children with the exception of one, perished in the flames of her cottage, the cries of the massacred mingling in her dying ears with the savage shouts of the fiendish murderers. The little girl eight years old, who escaped was sent back by the Dutch to New England, where a good many of her descendants live.

It was the custom of the Indians to take the name of a person they had killed, and the chief who led this attack called himself after the massacre, "Anne's Hoeck," which is ground for the belief that the great chief himself was her murderer. The neck of land at Pelham, N. Y., bears to this day the name of Anne's Hoeck or Anne's Hook.

This brave woman's death was the end of the theological tragedy of early Boston, but it was the beginning of that religious freedom we enjoy to-day.

MARGARET BRENT

Not long after King Charles made the grant of land to his friend, Lord Baltimore, a woman of queenly daring and republican courage found her way to the new colony and into the councils of its leading men, and her name, Margaret

Brent, stands for the most vigorous force in the early history of Maryland. She was born in England, about 1600, and died at Saint Mary's, Maryland, about 1661. A writer of this time has said about her, "Had she been born a queen she would have been as brilliant and daring as Elizabeth; had she been born a man she would have been a Cromwell in her courage and audacity."

However, she might not have exerted quite so much influence over these first Maryland colonies had she not stood in the relationship she did to the Governor of Maryland, Leonard Calvert, the brother of Lord Baltimore. There are some who think that Margaret Brent was an intimate friend or kinswoman of Leonard Calvert, and there are others who believe that she was his sweetheart. But at any rate an atmosphere of doubt and mystery still lingers about the names of Margaret Brent and Leonard Calvert and their old-time relationship.

It was in the year 1634, that Leonard Calvert came to America bringing over three hundred colonists, some twenty of them men of wealth and position. These three hundred English colonists sailed into wide Chesapeake Bay and up that broad river, the Potomac, till they reached the place where a little river joins the waters of the larger, and there they founded their city, calling both city and river Saint Mary's.

Four years after the coming of Leonard Calvert, Margaret Brent arrived in the city of Saint Mary's. It was in November, that Mistress Margaret first saw Maryland, then brilliant in the beauty of Indian Summer. The orioles were still singing in the forests, the red wild flowers were blooming in the crevices of the rocks and the trees still kept their foliage of red and gold, and the English woman is said to have remarked that the air of her new home was "Like the breath of Heaven;" that she had entered "Paradise."

Margaret, with her brothers and sisters, seem always to have had a prominent part in the affairs of the colony. Immediately after their arrival they took up land in the town and on Kent Island built themselves a Manor House and carried on a prosperous business. Margaret became as wise as her brothers or even wiser in the intricacy of the English law. We hear of her registering cattle marks, buying and selling property and signing herself "Attorney for My Brother." The early records of the American Colony afford rare glimpses of Mistress Margaret Brent as a person of influence and power. She was indeed a woman of pronounced courage and executive ability. She knew people and was able to manage them and their affairs with remarkable tact. Moreover, although she was no longer very young, she could still please and fascinate, and so it is not surprising that she became in effect if not in fact the woman ruler of Maryland. She is supposed to have shared the exile of Governor Calvert when rebellion drove him from the colony, but with fearlessness and daring she seems to have appeared in the colony at the time when her home was threatened by raids under Clayborne, the claimant of Kent Island. Two years passed before Governor Calvert was able to put down the rebellion and return to his colony and he did not live long to enjoy the peace that followed. He died in the summer of 1647, and there was wondering as to whom he would appoint his heir. Thomas Green, with a few others of the Governor's council, and Margaret Brent were with him just before he died. He named Thomas Green as his successor as Governor. Then his eyes rested upon Margaret Brent, perhaps with love, perhaps with confidence and admiration. There was no one in the colony so wise, so able, so loyal as she. Leonard Calvert had always known that. Pointing to her, so that all might see and understand, he made the will that has come down to us as the shortest one on record: "I make you my sole executrix," he said, "Take all, and pay all." And after he had spoken those words of laconic instruction, he asked that all would leave him except Mistress Margaret. One cannot know what passed between Leonard Calvert and Margaret Brent in this last interview, nor what they said, for Margaret Brent never told.

But, "Take all and pay all," he had said, and Margaret Brent determined to carry out his command to the letter. The first thing that she took was his house. There was some dispute as to her title to it, but Mistress Margaret did not wait for this dispute to close; she at once established herself in the Governor's mansion, for she was well acquainted with the old letter by which possession is nine points. Then having secured the house she collected all of Governor Calvert's property and took it under her care and management.

This would have been enough for most women but Mistress Margaret was not so easily satisfied. She was determined to have all that was implied in the phrase, "Take all and pay all," so we soon find her making claim that since she had been appointed "Executrix" of Leonard Calvert, she had the right to succeed Leonard Calvert as Lord Baltimore's attorney and in that character to receive all the profits and to pay all the debts of his lordship's estate and to attend to the state's reservation.

Her next step was more daring than all those that had gone before, being no less than a demand for vote and representation. This demand was made two centuries and a half ago, when talk of Woman's Rights was as unheard of as the steam engine or electricity. Certainly Margaret Brent was far in advance of her times. She might be known to history as the Original Suffragette! Her audacity carried her even further. She was Leonard Calvert's executrix, she told herself, and was entitled to vote in that capacity and so she concluded she had the right to two votes in the general assembly. No one but Margaret Brent would have meditated those two votes, one for a foreign Lord, who had never authorized her to act for him, and the other for a dead man whose only instruction to her had been, "Take all and pay all." We can only wonder at her ingenious reasoning, as did that biographer of hers who was moved to exclaim in admiration of her daring, "What woman would ever have dreamed of such a thing!"

Her astonishing stand for woman's rights was made on the 21st of January, 1648. At the first beat of the drum, that was used to call the assemblymen together in the early days of the Maryland colony, Mistress Margaret started on her way for Fort Saint John's, where the general assembly was to meet. We may well believe there was determination in her eye and in her attitude as she sat erect upon her horse and rode over the four miles of snow-covered roads to the fort, for she was determined that at least she would have her say before the crowd and show the justice of her suit. Mistress Margaret would not let herself be disturbed by the cool reception with which she was met; for, although the court tried to hedge her about with rules and orders to keep her quiet, she remained firm in her intentions to speak. And finally when her opportunity came she rose and put forward for the first time in America the claims of a woman's right to seat and vote in a legislative assembly.

We can only imagine the scene that followed that brief and dangerous speech of hers in the court room at Fort Saint John's. A wave of startled wonder and amazement passed over the whole assembly and preposterous as her demand was to those first Maryland planters, there were some among them who moved by her persuasive eloquence would have been willing to grant her request. But Governor Green, who had always regarded Margaret Brent as his most dangerous rival, braced himself for prompt and autocratic action and promptly refused. The Maryland records attest, "The said Mistress Brent should have no vote in the house." The "said Mistress Brent" did not take her defeat without protest. She objected vehemently to the proceedings of the assembly and departed from the court room in anger and dignity. She had failed in her purpose but by her bold stand she had made for herself the signal record as the first woman in America to advocate her right to vote. It is to be noted, moreover, that the Governor Green who had denied her this right was the Governor who turned to her for help whenever an emergency arose.

Soon after the death of Leonard Calvert there threatened to be a mutiny in the army. The soldiers who had fought for

Governor Calvert when he was an exile in Virginia had been promised that they should be paid in full "out of the stock and personal property of his Lordship's plantation." Governor Calvert was dead, the pay was not forthcoming and the only course left to the soldiers seemed to be insurrection. Governor Green could think of nothing to appease the half-starved indignant troops, so he went to Margaret Brent for aid. As soon as Mistress Margaret heard of the trouble, she recalled the instructions which Leonard Calvert had given her to "pay all," so without hesitation she sold the cattle belonging to Lord Baltimore and paid off all the hungry soldiers. News traveled slowly in those early Colonial days and it was some time before Lord Baltimore heard of all that Margaret Brent was claiming and doing as his own attorney and executrix of his brother. And not really knowing Mistress Margaret he was inclined to look upon her as a person who had been "meddling" in his affairs and he wrote "tartly" and with "bitter invectives" concerning her to the general assembly. But the general assembly understood Margaret Brent better than Lord Baltimore did and they sent a spirited reply to him in gallant praise of Margaret Brent and her wise conduct. So we find the Maryland Assembly which could not give Mistress Margaret the right to vote defending her even against the Lord of their own colony and declaring her "the ablest man among them."

To the end of her days Margaret Brent continued to lead a life of ability and energetic action. There are occasional glimpses of her latter history as she flashes across the records of the Maryland colony—always a clear-cut, fearless, vigorous personality. At one time she appears before the assembly claiming that the tenements belonging to Lord Calvert's manor should be under her guard and management. Again she comes pleading her cause against one Thomas Gerard for five thousand pounds of tobacco. At another time she figures as an offender accused of stealing and selling cattle only to retort indignantly that the cattle were her own, and to demand a trial by jury. In all of these cases and many others she seems to have had her own way. The General Assembly never denied her anything but the right to vote. She had only to express a wish in her clear persuasive fashion and it was granted. In point of view Margaret Brent ruled the colony.

When she came for the last time before the General Assembly her hair must have been gray, but her speech no less eloquent, and her manner no less charming, than in the days of Leonard Calvert. We can imagine her in the presence of the court stating with dignity and frankness that she was the heir to Thomas White, a Maryland gentleman, who, dying, left her his whole estate as a proof of "his love and affection and of his constant wish to marry her." One would like to know more about this Thomas, but he appears only in the one role, that of Margaret Brent's lover. It has been suggested that possibly if Mr. White had lived, Mistress Margaret might have been induced at last to resign her independent state; that she had grown weary of her land operations and her duties as executrix and attorney and was willing to settle down to a life of domestic calm. But it is almost impossible to think of Margaret Brent as changing her business-like, self-reliant nature and meditating matrimony. It is more likely that this interesting and unusual Colonial dame died as she had lived, loving nothing but the public good and the management of her own and other people's affairs.

MOLLY BRANDT

No pen picture has been left of Molly Brandt, and yet her influence had much to do with the colonists' success in subduing the most savage of the Indian tribes. She was the sister of Joseph Brandt, that mysterious character who was supposed to have been born an Indian chief among the Mohawk tribe, and who was the young Nation's intermediary with the Indians. It was through her shrewdness and the influential position which

35

Molly Brandt came to occupy in the family of Sir William Johnson that her brother came to the attention of those in authority and received his education. She arranged to have him sent to the Moor Charity School at Lebanon, Connecticut, in 1761. Through this training of his mind, and the cultivation of sympathy with the colonists, he became as valuable an assistant as many trained diplomatists have been in later years. We find, moreover, that in 1770, Sir William, after the decease of Lady Johnson, "took to his home as his wife, Mary Brandt, or Miss Molly." And this may be the first historic instance of an American girl marrying a title!

MARY MOORE

The early history of West Virginia is filled with the same stories of privation, suffering, and horrors experienced by the settlers in Tennessee, Kentucky, and North Carolina. The privations of that time necessitated women taking upon themselves the hardest labors. They worked with their husbands clearing the land, and the rude provisions for domestic comfort were largely those acquired by their own efforts. The tableware of those days consisted of a few pewter plates and kettles which had survived long journeys from the East. They wove the cloth of which their own and their children's garments were made, spun the flax which made the linen, and in fact, the entire furnishings of their homes were the work of their own hands. It is said that the first settlers came into West Virginia in 1749, and in 1751 two settlers were sent in by the Green Brier Company to open up the lands, and the first settlement was made near Wheeling. As soon as the outposts were established, others followed in the train of these first venturesome pioneers. In 1761, Mrs. Dennis was taken captive from the James' settlement and taken to the Indian settlement near Chillicothe, Ohio. She became famous among the Indians as a nurse, and her medicines, prepared from herbs, were sought far and near, and through this medium she ultimately made her escape. In 1763, while gathering herbs she reached the Ohio River. Wandering alone through the woods and the forests, and rafting herself down the great Kanawha, she ultimately reached the Green Brier, but was so exhausted and worn by her long tramp and the exposure that she finally gave up and lay down expecting to die, but was discovered by some of the settlers and nursed and cared for. But for this act of kindness the settlers were made to pay dearly. They were attacked by the Indians, and all the men were killed and the women and children taken captives. In this attack a Mrs. Clendennin showed such courage that her name has been enrolled among the women heroes of that time. Early in 1778, an attack was made on one of the blockhouses on the upper Monongahela. In this hand to hand conflict, Mrs. Cunningham, the wife of Edward Cunningham, seeing her husband's strength almost spent, grabbed the tomahawk and finished the Indian who would have taken her husband's life. In an attack by the Indians on the house of William Morgan, in Dunker's Bottom, Mrs. Morgan was bound to a tree. She succeeded in untying herself with her teeth and escaping with her child. In March, 1781, an attack was made by the Indians on the house of Captain John Thomas, situated on one of the little streams tributary to the Monongahela. Captain Thomas was killed and Mrs. Thomas and her six children butchered by the savages, only one little boy escaping. While this bloody orgy was going on, a woman named Elizabeth Juggins, who had been attracted by the cries of the helpless victims, had come to their aid. On reaching the house, she realized her absolute helplessness and hid under one of the beds. When the Indians had left, supposing that they had completed their murderous work, Miss Juggins found that Mrs. Thomas was still alive, and succeeded in ultimately reaching other settlers and spreading the alarm. On the 29th of June, 1785, the house of Mr. Scott was attacked. Mrs. Scott witnessed the savages cutting the throats of three of her children and the murder of her husband, and then was carried into captivity by the Indians. The old chief seemed to have at least a drop of the milk of human kindness in his veins, and Mrs. Scott through the care of the old man succeeded in gaining her liberty. She wandered from the 10th of July to the nth of August through the woods with nothing on which to sustain life but the juices of plants. Among this long list of names of the women who suffered Indian captivity and its attendant horrors were the names of Mrs. Glass, Mary Moore, Martha Evans, and other splendid women. James Moore, Mary Moore's brother, was taken captive by the Indians in 1784, and in 1786, a party of Indians made a hasty attack on the settlement before they were able to realize their danger, the settlers having been lulled into a feeling of security by the absence of any trouble for some time. Her father was killed in this attack, and her mother and three children—two brothers and a sister—were made prisoners. They were taken into the Scioto Valley, and here Mary Moore and her friend, Martha Evans, spent some time in captivity. They were ultimately sold to men in the neighborhood of Detroit, where they were employed as servants. In the invasion of Logan from Kentucky three years later, a young French trader took a great fancy to young James Moore, who was living among the Indians of the Pow Wow Society, and through this trader, James obtained information of his sister Mary, who was then near Detroit. Young Moore went to Stogwell's place, where he found his sister had been very cruelly treated and was then in the most frightful condition of poverty and suffering. James applied to the commanding officer of Detroit, who sent him to Colonel McKee, then superintendent for the Indians, and Stogwell was brought to trial through the complaint made against him by James Moore. It was decided that Mary Moore could be returned to her home when proper remuneration was made, and through the efforts of Thomas Evans, the brother of Martha who had accompanied Mary Moore into captivity, she obtained her liberty in 1789, after having suffered three years of captivity.

Shortly after her return to Rockridge, Mary Moore went to live with her uncle, Joseph Walker, whose home was near Lexington, and she later became the wife of Rev. Samuel Brown, pastor of New Providence. She was the mother of eleven children, nine of whom survived her. Martha Evans married a man by the name of Hummer and resided in Indiana, rearing a large family of children.

During the attack of Cornwallis and his approach near Charlotte, a Mr. Brown sought protection in the home of James Haines, and while here the British plundered the house and made the owner a prisoner. Mrs. Haines' maiden name was Annie Huggins. She was the daughter of John Huggins, a Scotch Presbyterian, who had emigrated to America from, the north of Ireland, in 1730. She had married, in 1788, James Haines, and in 1792, he with his two brothers had emigrated to a colony in North Carolina, and here they were neighbors to the hostile Cherokees and Kanawhas who gave the settlers of those days constant alarm and terror. Later Colonel Bird, of the British army, established Fort Chissel as a protection to these settlers, and still later Governor Dobbs, of North Carolina, established Fort Loudon in the very heart of the Cherokee Nation. These settlements grew rapidly, notwithstanding the close proximity of these savage Indians. One of the striking characteristics of almost all these settlers of that time was their strong religious faith, particularly the women, and certainly nothing else could have supported and sustained them through the daily horrors of their lives. Mrs. Haines died in 1790, having survived her husband only a few years.

ELIZABETH BARTHOLOMEW

Born in Bethlehem, Hunterdon County, New Jersey, February 14, 1749, she was the sixteenth child of her parents, having even a younger sister. On her mother's side she was descended from the Huguenots of France. Her parents had removed to Germany after the Edict of Nantes, and later emigrated to America. In 1771 Elizabeth Bartholomew was married to Alexander Harper, of Harpersfield, New York. He was one of several brothers to enter the service at the outbreak of the Revolutionary War. Owing to the frequent visits of the Indians and Tories, the families of these Whig leaders were obliged to seek protection in Fort Schoharie. In moments of peace and quiet, Mrs. Harper lived with her children a short distance from the fort. In times of trouble, she spent her necessary imprisonment within the enclosure of the fort in baking bread for the soldiers and in making bullets. On one of these occasions the commander of the fort becoming discouraged by the tardy arrival of ammunition decided to surrender, and ordered a flag of truce hoisted. This brought forth such indignant protests from Mrs. Harper and the other women who had been working since early morning preparing ammunition for the poor wearied soldiers, that they determined to make one more effort to repel the enemy themselves. A soldier offered to fire on the flag of truce if hoisted, provided the women would conceal him, and as often as the flag was run up he fired at it, bringing down the wrath of the commander, who was unable to find the audacious person who treated his authority with such contempt. This delay and the insubordination of the soldiers prevented the truce being carried into effect and the reinforcement arrived in time to force the retreat of the enemy. In 1780, Captain Harper, finding no necessity, owing to the peaceful condition then prevailing, of his longer service, went to look after his property in Harpersfield. Here he was taken prisoner by the Indians and carried to Canada, Mrs. Harper being in ignorance of his capture. He was eventually released. In 1797, a company was formed in Harpersfield to purchase land in the far West, or what is better known as the Northwest Territory. The Connecticut Land Company was formed, and people were sent out to investigate the new country. On the 7th of March, 1798, Alexander Harper,

William McFarland, and Ezra Gregory started for this new land of promise with their families. After a most difficult trip they reached, on the 28th of June, Cunningham's Creek, and near here Colonel Harper took up his location near Unionville. This little settlement was rapidly added to by their friends from the East. In March, Daniel Bartholomew brought out his family accompanied by Judge Griswold, and what is now Ashtabula was settled in a township called Richfield. In August an election was held for the purpose of sending an application to the convention to be held at Chillicothe the following winter preparatory to an effort for the admission of Ohio as a state into the Union. In the war of 1812, the country was exposed to all the dangers of the frontier. Mrs. Harper lived to the great age of eighty-five, dying on the 11th of June, 1833, retaining her remarkable intellect to the very last.

MARY DUNLEVY

Mary Dunlevy was of Scotch parentage, being born on the voyage of her parents from Scotland to America, in 1765. The family name was Craig. They settled in New York and experienced the early oppressions which brought on the Revolution. Her father's death occurred soon after they reached this country, her mother being left with the care of a little family of three—two daughters and one son. At the time of the occupation of New York City by the British troops, Mrs. Craig expressed no little alarm for the safety of herself and children. Among her small circle of friends from the old country was a British officer, whom she married. This made a very uncomfortable home life for Mary Dunlevy, who soon sought a more friendly atmosphere in the home of Dr. Halstead, of Elizabethtown, New Jersey. She was a strong advocate of Independence and in this respect was in sympathy with those of her new home and felt deeply the separation from her family. Her sister married an Englishman

41

and went to England to live, but Mary always felt the warmest friendship for her American friends, and frequently risked her life in efforts to save their property from destruction by appealing to the British Commander, and on one occasion a sword was drawn upon her threatening instant death if she did not leave the room of this austere commanding officer. She, however, persisted and did ultimately accomplish her purpose and save the property of her friends. Frequently she spent whole days and nights making bullets and tending the wounded and dying. She was one of the young girls who witnessed the triumphal march of General Washington and helped to strew the road with flowers as he passed. There was no more enthusiastic participant in the rejoicing over the establishment of independence than Mary Dunlevy. In 1789, she married James Carpenter, who had recently returned from a visit of exploration to the new Northwest Territory. He was so delighted with the new country that he determined to settle there, and thither they went after their marriage in 1789. They made their home near Maysville, Kentucky. Mary had been accustomed to hardship and exposure in her early days and proved her worth in this new home. But Carpenter's difficult labors of the winter in clearing the ground and raising the building which was to form their little home brought on a hemorrhage which two years later resulted in his death. Though urged by her friends to take up her home inside the borders which the settlers had erected, she preferred the solitude and independence of her own little home which her husband had made for her. It is said that she planned a way of protecting her little children in case of an attack by the Indians by digging out beneath the puncheon floor of her cabin a small cellar, and every night she lifted the timbers and placed her children on beds in this cellar, keeping a lonely vigil herself. Her fears were not groundless, her cabin being frequently surrounded by savages, and but for her careful provisions for protection, she and her little family no doubt would have been killed. Cincinnati became the headquarters of the army through the establishment of a garrison there known as Fort Washington. One of the first schools established in the Northwest Territory was that of young Francis Dunlevy who had served in many Indian campaigns, and came to Columbia, in 1792, and established his school. Hearing of Mrs. Carpenter's courage and sacrifices for her children, he sought her out and finding that none of them had been exaggerated he became a suitor for her hand, and they were married in January, 1793. Mr. Dunlevy became one of the most respected citizens of that section of the country, and was afterwards a member of the legislature of the Northwest Territory and the convention which formed the constitution of Ohio. He was also Judge of the Court of Common Pleas. Mrs. Dunlevy had two daughters by her first marriage and three sons and three daughters by her second, and after the death of her eldest child her health failed and she died in 1828, without any apparent cause but that of a broken heart.

RUTH SPARKS

Ruth Sparks, whose maiden name was Ruth Sevier, was the daughter of General John Sevier by his second wife, Catherine Sherrill. General Sevier commanded his troops through the Indian wars, and proved the greatest friend and protector of the settlement. General Sevier was most successful in his dealings with the Indians, and during the intervals of peace, the chiefs of the tribes were often seen at his house. Ruth always manifested the greatest interest in the Indian history and lives. At one time General Sevier had thirty Indian prisoners at his house, whom he fed and cared for at his own expense, and through this kindness the greatest friendship was shown him by the neighboring tribes, and Ruth learned from them the Cherokee language. The Indians always predicted that she would some day be a chief's wife, and strange as it may seem, this was really fulfilled. In the early settling of Kentucky, many bloody conflicts had taken place between the Indians and the white settlers, and during one of these a white child four years of age was captured by the Indians and taken to the Shawnee settlement on the Kentucky River. The old chief of the Shawnees had two sons about the age of this young white captive, whom he immediately adopted as a son, and he was reared with them, his name changed to Shawtunte. After his release from captivity, he was given the name of Richard Sparks. Here he lived until he had reached the age of sixteen, becoming almost an Indian in his habits and, of course, knew no other language, he having been taken when so young among them. In 1794 he was released and returned to Kentucky just before the victories of General Wayne over the Indians. On his return none of his relatives recognized him, and he was only recognized by his mother by a small mark on his body. Sparks sought the aid and protection of General Sevier, who found his knowledge and experience of the Indians most valuable. General Sevier used his influence to procure for him a military appointment, and he was given a captain's commission. He performed very valuable service for General Wayne, and stood very high among all the officers. He met Ruth Sevier, and won her love and the ultimate consent of the Governor for her marriage to this untutored young man. She found him a very apt scholar, and he was soon able to pass the examination which enabled him to be promoted to the rank of colonel in the United States army, being ordered to Fort Pickering on the Mississippi, now the beautiful city of Memphis. This was one of the chain of forts established to maintain peace among the Chickasaw Indians. After the purchase of Louisiana, Colonel Sparks was moved to New Orleans. Mrs. Sparks proved a most valuable helpmeet and aid to her husband, performing the duties of his secretary, keeping his accounts, writing his letters, and making out his reports to the War Department. Owing to his early life among the Indians and General Sevier's well-known reputation of humanity, both Colonel and Mrs. Sparks had a most beneficial influence over the Indians of the lower Mississippi. Colonel Sparks' health failed, and he was at first allowed to return to Mrs. Sparks' old home, but they finally removed to Staunton, Virginia, at which place he died in 1815. Mrs. Sparks married the second time a wealthy planter of Mississippi, and lived near Port Gibson in Mississippi. While on a visit in 1874 to some friends in Maysville, Kentucky, she died.

SARAH SHELBY

Was the daughter of Mrs. Bledsoe who was so famous among the settlers of the first settlements of Tennessee. Sarah was quite young when her parents moved from Virginia to eastern Tennessee. Miss Bledsoe married in 1784, David Shelby. Mrs. Shelby's husband was said to be the first merchant in Nashville, in 1790. Mrs. Shelby suffered all the exposures and hardships incident to the life of the early settlers in Tennessee.

RUHAMA GREENE

Ruhama Greene was born in Jefferson County, Virginia, and married Charles Builderback and they were among the first settlers on the Ohio near Wheeling. In an attack made by the Indians, in 1789, on this settlement, Mrs. Builderback and her husband were taken prisoners. She remained a prisoner about nine months, being condemned to the hardest labor in working for the squaws and their brutal masters. She was finally released by the commandant at Fort Washington, and restored to her family. After her husband's death, she married a Mr. John Greene, and removed to a settlement near Lancaster, where she resided at the time of her death in 1842.

REBECCA ROUSE

Among the settlers to remove from New England, in 1788, to Ohio, we find the names of John Rouse and Jonathan Duvall. John Rouse's family consisted of a wife and eight children. Mrs. Duvall was the sister of Mrs. Rouse, and he was the "noble architect of the Mayflower," which conveyed the first detachment from Simrels Ferry, on the Yohoghany to the mouth of Muskingum and was among the first settlers to land on the 7th of April, 1788, in the state of Ohio. The large covered wagons which the settlers used in those days for conveying their families across the country were called schooners and frequently received nautical names. Teams of oxen were frequently preferred to horses by these Nw England emigrants and pioneers, they being more familiar with their use and, too, they were less likely to be captured by the Indians, as, owing to the slowness of their gait they were not considered desirable possessions by these warrior inhabitants. Thus outfitted, this little band of emigrants made their way from New England through New York, Pennsylvania, and over the mountain ranges to Ohio. As they approached the mountains the rains of November had set in and their progress was filled with the greatest difficulties and hardships particularly to the women and children, who were obliged to walk most of the way over the rocky and steep ascent of the mountain roads. Near the last of November when they reached the point where the Monongahela and the Alleghany meet in the waters of the Ohio, they rested after their terrible struggles through the mountains. The old garrison Fort Pitt was then standing as a protection to the few hundred inhabitants. While their boats in which they had come down the Monongahela were moored the waters rose, and the men rushing to the rescue, the entire party was carried down the river to a point called Fort Mackintosh at the mouth of the Beaver and to the new settlement at Muskingum. Here they embarked for a place known as Buffalo, to which point some of their friends from the East had preceded them. The following spring a company was formed and a settlement established on the Ohio River called Belpre, and here Captain Duvall, Mr. Rouse, and several other settlers, joined by many from New England, moved their families. In 1790, Bathsheba Rouse opened a school for boys and girls at Belpre, which is believed to be the first school for white children in the state of Ohio. Bathsheba Rouse married Richard Greene, the son of Griffin Greene, one of the Ohio Company's agents. Cynthia Rouse became the wife of Hon. Paul Fearing, the first delegate to Congress from the Northwest Territory and for many years a judge of the court. Levi Barber, a receiver of public moneys and a member of Congress for two sessions, was the husband of Elizabeth Rouse. These early settlers were the founders of the state of Ohio. Many of these settlers of the Northwest Territory were men in the prime of life who had exhausted their fortunes in the War of Independence, and being left in the most impoverished condition, had chosen to seek their fortunes in the new country west of the Alleghanies. Many of the young men were the descendants of the Revolutionary patriots who had given their lives for their country. The Moravian school at Bethlehem at this time enjoyed quite a reputation. We find among these early settlers one Colonel Ebenezer Sproat who had been a distinguished officer of the Revolution. His daughter, Sarah W. Sproat, was born in Providence, Rhode Island, on the 28th of January, 1782. Her grandfather was Commodore Abram Whipple, also a distinguished hero of that war, who impoverished himself for his country in fitting out vessels and men for its service. His son-in-law and he, finding their necessities great, joined the emigrants to the new settlement near Marietta. When but ten years of age, Miss Sproat was sent to Bethlehem school, and after three years to Philadelphia to complete her education. In 1797, her father went to Philadelphia to bring her home and brought with them a piano, the first taken west of the Alleghany Mountains. After the establishment of the Northwest Territory, they had what was called a general court, which met alternately at Cincinnati, Detroit, and Marietta. Among the young lawyers practicing before this court was one Mr. Sibley who had come from Massachusetts to Ohio in 1787, and resided at that time in Detroit. While attending one of the sessions of this court, he met Miss Sproat. Their friendship ripening into love, they were married in October, 1802. At that time the route from Marietta to Detroit was by way of the Ohio River to Pittsburgh, thence to Erie and across the lake to Detroit. This city was largely settled by Southerners and many French who were the descendants of noble families in France, making at that time a society of much refinement and polish. Colonel Sproat was one of the most distinguished men of that section of the country, and the family have in their possession a miniature of him painted by Kosciuszko, the distinguished Pole and himself having been intimate friends in the Revolution. In February, 1805, Colonel Sproat died, and in June of that year the city of Detroit was entirely destroyed by fire. Mrs. Sibley had been spending the winter with her father and mother, owing to his failing health. Colonel Sibley fitted up as soon as possible a very large old house which was then situated some distance from the town, now the very center of the city opposite the Biddle house, and here they made their home for many years. At the time of the war of 1812, Mrs. Sibley bore herself with great courage and rendered great assistance, making cartridges and scraping lint for the wounded. At the time of the news of the surrender the humiliation felt by these courageous women was shown by an incident of which Mrs. Dyson, a cousin of Mrs. Sibley, was the heroine. As the American soldiers marched out of the fort, Mrs. Dyson took all the clothing and belongings, tied them up in a bundle, and threw them out of the window, declaring that the British should not have them. Mrs. Sibley applied to General Proctor after the surrender for permission to go to her family in Ohio, and this was finally granted her, and in the spring when Detroit was again given up to the Americans, she returned to her home. On the death of her grandparents,

Commodore and Mrs. Whipple, in 1819, Mrs. Sproat was left entirely alone, so Mrs. Sibley made the journey to Marietta most of the way on horseback to remove her mother to Detroit, where she remained until her death in 1832. Mrs. Sibley's husband, Solomon Sibley, was one of the judges of the Supreme Court of the early territory of Michigan, and on his removal to Detroit he was made one of the first members of the territorial legislature. He was also United States commissioner and helped General Cass to negotiate the treaty with the Indians in which they surrendered a large portion of the peninsula of Michigan. He was a delegate from the territory of Michigan in Congress, District Attorney of the United States, and Judge of the Supreme Court of Michigan. He died on April 4, 1846, one of the most highly respected citizens of Detroit.

ANN BAILEY

The Scioto Company early in 1786 sent out a prospectus of their lands in the Northwest Territory. A glowing account was given of the opportunities for settlers, and an office for the sale of these lands was opened in Paris, France. Many of the French families had been driven out of their native country by the Revolution and this seemed to offer them an opportunity of regaining their fortune. Some five or six hundred emigrants including men of all professions who had purchased lands through the agent in Paris, sailed in February, 1790, from Havre de Grace for Alexandria, Virginia. Here they were received with a warm welcome, but soon discovered that the company had failed in their requirements by the United States Government, and that the lands had reverted to the Treasury Board and had been sold in 1787 pursuant to an act of Congress passed the July preceding. Realizing their situation, a meeting was called and a committee appointed to go to New York and demand indemnification from the acting agents of the Scioto Company, and another committee was appointed to appeal personally to General Washington to right their wrongs. Finally an agreement was reached that other lands should be secured to them and that the site of Gallipolis should be surveyed and parcelled out in lots, houses erected, and wagons and supplies furnished to convey the colonists to Ohio. But many had lost their faith in the company, and they removed to New York, Philadelphia, and elsewhere. The few who still held on to the hope of obtaining some foothold in the new country set out as soon as the wagons and necessary supplies could be secured, reaching their destination in October, 1790. Here they found cabins erected, block houses for the protection against an attack, and many other things for their comfort. They set to work at once clearing the land, and in 1791 a party started out to explore the country adjoining and they hoped that on their return the Scioto Company would put them in possession of the lands which they had purchased, but being convinced of the hopelessness of this, they petitioned Congress for an appropriation of land, which resulted in twenty thousand acres being turned over to be equally divided among the French emigrants living at Gallipolis at a certain time under condition of their remaining there a certain number of years. Other grants were afterwards given to these colonists in Kentucky. In the history of this settlement we find the account of a most remarkable woman who received from the settlers the name of "Mad Ann." Her maiden name was Hennis. She was born at Liverpool, and married a man by the name of Richard Trotter. Richard Trotter volunteered as one of the men under General Lewis, who went out at the order of Lord Dunmore, the Governor of Virginia, in 1774, against the Indian towns on the Scioto, and while waiting for news from the commander-in-chief at Point Pleasant an engagement between the Indians and these troops took place in which the Virginians suffered great loss. Among those engaged in this battle were the well-known names of Shelby, Sevier, and James Robertson, spoken of in former accounts. Trotter was killed in this battle.

From the time of the news of her husband's death, Ann Bailey seemed possessed of a wild spirit of revenge. She abandoned all female employment and even gave up female attire, clad herself in hunting shirt, moccasins, wore a knife and tomahawk, and carried a gun. Notwithstanding her strange conduct and the assumption of manly habits, she made a second alliance. She went with a body of soldiers which were to form a garrison at a fort on the great Kanawha where Charlestown is now located, and we find in many of the historical sketches she is spoken of as handling firearms with such expertness that she frequently carried off the prize. She became a trusted messenger, taking long journeys on horseback entirely alone. One incident is told of how, when information of a supposed attack on a fort at Charlestown was threatened, and the commandant found it necessary to send to Camp Union near Lewisburg for supplies, as they were without ammunition, Ann Bailey offered to make this journey of one hundred miles through a trackless forest alone. Her offer was accepted and she reached Camp Union in safety, delivered her orders and returned as she had come, alone, laden with the ammunition. It is said that the commandant stated that the fort would not have been saved except for this act of heroism on the part of Mrs. Bailey, which hardly has a parallel. The services she rendered during the war endeared her to the people who overlooked her eccentricities and were ever ready to extend to her every kindness which their gratitude suggested. When her son settled in Gallipolis, she came with him and spent the remainder of her life wandering about the country, fishing and hunting. Her death took place in 1825.

Among the incidents of the early settlement of Kentucky none is more significant than the Rustic Parliament, which convened at Boonesborough, May 24, 1775. Without any warrant other than a common desire and reverence for justice, seventeen delegates convened. They were five hundred miles from any organized society or civil government. Nominally within the jurisdiction of Virginia, nominally subjects of the British crown, without knowledge of the battles of Lexington and Concord or even the Declaration of Independence, coming into the wilderness without a charter, they proceeded to the enactment of laws for the establishment of the courts of justice for their common defense, for the collection of debts, for the punishment of crime, for the restraint of vice. Having no early education, knowing only the meaning of the word "duty," they proceeded to express it in the laws made. The names of these worthy delegates were: Squire Boone, Daniel Boone, Samuel Henderson, William Moore, Richard Callaway, Thomas Slaughter, John Lythe, Valentine Harmon, James Harrod, Nathan Hammond, Isaac Hite, Azariah David, John Todd, Alexander Spotswood Dandridge, John Floyd, and Samuel Wood.

REBECCA BRYANT BOONE

The wife of Daniel Boone, born about 1755 in the Yadkin settlement of western North Carolina, and her daughter Jemima, are supposed to be the first white women residents of Kentucky. In 1773, in company with her husband, she set out for their new home. It is believed that no women suffered more hardships or showed more heroism than these two white women, the first to enter Kentucky. This little band was attacked by Indians in the mountains, and six men of the party were killed, among them her eldest son. They took up their home in the Valley of the Clinch River, where they lived until 1775. Daniel Boone had undertaken a surveying trip for the Government extending from tidewater to the Falls of the Ohio, a distance of about eight hundred miles. After attending the Rustic Parliament, he returned to Clinch River and brought his family back to Boonesborough. In February, 1778, Daniel Boone was captured by the Indians while out trying to secure a supply of salt. He was carried north of the Ohio River, and all tidings of him to his family ceased. His wife, of course, supposed he had been killed, and taking her children, she returned to Yadkin, North Carolina. In 1778, Boone escaped and returned to Boonesborough, joining his family the following autumn and bringing them into Kentucky in 1780. In 1782 another son was killed in a massacre by the Indians. Mrs. Boone died in 1813, leaving a record of heroism unequalled by any woman of that time, living as she had, much of her time alone and constantly surrounded by savages, her life and that of her children in constant peril. Kentucky has shown its appreciation of this heroism and her part in the early history of the state by the legislature passing a resolution to bring her remains and those of her husband back to the state and burying them with honor at Frankfort.

KETURAH LEITCH TAYLOR

Keturah Leitch Taylor, formerly Keturah Moss, was born September 11, 1773, in Goochland County, Virginia. She was the daughter of Major Hugh Moss of the Revolutionary Army. Her father having died in 1784, she, with two sisters, was brought to Kentucky by her uncle, Rev. Augustine Eastin, their mother having married again. While en route to Kentucky, the train of settlers of which they were a part, was attacked by Indians, and many were killed. This was witnessed by Keturah Moss, then only a child of fifteen years. Her early experiences and her courage make her one of the cherished memories of Kentucky, and her descendants are among the well-known names of that state.

SUSANNA HART SHELBY

Susanna Hart was born in Caswell County, North Carolina, February 18, 1761, and died at Traveler's Rest, Lincoln County, Kentucky, June 19, 1833, aged seventy-two years. She was the daughter of Captain Nathan Hart and Sarah Simpson. The Harts were very wealthy people for those early times. His brother Thomas was the father of Mrs. Henry Clay. The three Harts, Nathan, David and Thomas, formed a company known as Henderson and Company, proprietors of the "Colony of Transylvania in America." This was a purchase from the Indians, and consisted of almost the entire state of Kentucky, but the legislature of Virginia made this transaction null and void, and gave them two hundred thousand acres of land, for which they paid ten thousand pounds sterling, for the important service they had rendered in opening the country. This is the company which first sent Daniel Boone to Kentucky; and he was the pioneer who opened up this country for them. In April, 1784, Sarah Hart was married to Colonel Isaac Shelby, who was afterwards the first governor of the state. He had seen distinguished service in the Revolutionary War, remaining with the army until after the capture of Cornwallis. While on a visit to Kentucky, in 1782, in the fort at Boonesborough, he met Susanna Hart, whose father had just a short time previous been killed by the Indians, leaving her an orphan. Their marriage took place in the stockade fort at Boonesborough. The hardships and bravery which these people showed and endured in the early settling in this part of the country, then a wilderness filled with savages, can hardly be appreciated by the present generation. Fitting tribute to such women should not be neglected, as they went as pioneers blazing the trail of civilization, spreading Christianity, which brought these sections into states, and made life in them possible and peaceful. Susanna Hart was the helpmeet of her husband, and in all the duties which devolved upon the wife and mother of those days—the spinning of the flax, the making of clothing, the entire labor of the home—were to her always a pleasant occupation. She was spoken of as a woman of most pleasing face, quiet and dignified presence, possessing the rare combination of extreme energy and great repose. She seemed a woman who could perform and endure, kind and helpful, a woman who retained to the last that gentle disposition and sweet nature which inspired confidence, of an even temperament, who retained to the last her beauty, and transmitted her charms to her descendants. She was the mother of ten children. Her life left her name one which Kentucky holds dear.

MARY HOPKINS CABELL BRECKENRIDGE

Was born in February, 1768, and died at Lexington. Kentucky, in 1858, aged ninety years. Her husband, Hon. John Breckenridge, was one of the noted men of Kentucky, and was appointed Attorney-General of the United States at one time. She is spoken of as a woman of great courage and remarkable character, and was the "founding mother" of a worthy and distinguished family. One of her daughters, Mary, married General David Castleman. of Kentucky, and Letitia Preston married General P. B. Porter, of Niagara Falls. One of her descendants was General Peter A. Porter, who fell in the assault on Coal Harbor. A granddaughter, Margaret E. Breckenridge, the daughter of Dr. John Breckenridge, was known during the Civil War as the "angel of the hospitals." It is reported she once said, "Shall men die by thousands for their country and no woman risk her life?"

HENRIETTA HUNT MORGAN

Daughter of Colonel John W. Hunt, and sister of Honorable Francis Keys Hunt, of Kentucky, was born in Lexington, Kentucky, in 1805, and died November 15, 1891. She married Governor Calvin C. Morgan, and was the mother of two of Kentucky's famous men, Colonel Calvin M. Morgan and General John Morgan. She had three other sons and two daughters, one of whom was the wife of General Basil W. Duke, and the other of General A. P. Hill.

SUSAN LUCY BARRY TAYLOR

Was born in Lexington, Kentucky, in 1807, and died at the old family mansion at Newport, Kentucky, December 8, 1881. She was among the first women who, even at the tender age of fifteen, made an appeal in one of her essays at school for the higher education of women. Her children were more or less famous in their own state.

MARY YELLOTT JOHNSTON

Formerly Mary Yellott Dashiell, was born September 13, 1806, and was a great-niece of the distinguished Governor Winder, of Maryland. She was connected with several of our most distinguished families, the Dashiells, Handys, Harrisons, Hancocks, Bayards, Randolphs, Warder and Percys.

MARGARET WICKLIFFE PRESTON

Margaret Wickliffe Preston one of the first "granddames" of the olden times, was born in Lexington, Kentucky, in 1819, and was the daughter of Robert Wickliffe, who gave his daughter every advantage which wealth, social position, and education could bring to her. Her husband was appointed minister to Spain, in 1858, and there she made a most favorable impression, by her culture, refinement, and grace of manner. Her conversational powers were always remarkable, and she was usually the center of attraction wherever she appeared. Her daughter married General Draper, of Massachusetts, who served in Congress and then as our minister to Italy, and Mrs. Draper's home in Washington is one of the social centers of to-day.

MARY BLEDSOE

One of the earliest pioneers of the colonial history of Kentucky. In 1758, Colonel Burd, of the British Army, established Fort Chissel, in Wythe County, Virginia, to protect the frontiers, and advancing into what is now Sullivan County, Tennessee, built a fort near Long Island on the Holston. There was not then a single white man living in the borders of Tennessee. At irregular intervals from 1765 to 1769, pioneer parties came from Virginia and North Carolina, forming settlements and stations. The country was one vast wilderness, its only inhabitants being buffaloes and all kinds of wild game, with the savage Indians making frequent raids, but the newcomers were not daunted by the situation, and here erected cabins, and constructed stockade forts against the attacks by the Indians. In 1769, at Fort Chissel, we find two Bledsoe brothers, Englishmen by birth. They soon pushed farther on into the valley of the Holston. This portion of the county, now Sullivan County, was supposed to be, at that time, within the limits of Virginia. The Bledsoes with the

Shelbys settled themselves here in this mountainous region. They suffered the severest privation and the greatest hardships in exploring the regions and establishing their little homes. During the first year not more than fifty families crossed the mountains, but others afterward came until the little settlement swelled to hundreds, and during the Revolutionary struggle, that region became the refuge of many patriots, driven by British invasion from Virginia, the Carolinas, and Georgia, some of their best families seeking homes there. Colonel Anthony Burd, an excellent surveyor, was appointed clerk to the commissioners who ran the line dividing Virginia and North Carolina. In June, 1776, he was chosen to command the militia of the county to repel the invasions and attacks of the savages and defend the frontier. The battle of Long Island, fought a few miles below Bledsoe Station, was one of the earliest and hardest fought battles in the history of Tennessee in those times. In 1779, Sullivan County was recognized as a part of North Carolina, and Anthony Bledsoe was appointed Colonel, and Isaac Shelby Lieutenant-Colonel of its military forces. Colonel Isaac Shelby, of whom we have spoken heretofore as the surveyor employed by the Henderson-Hart Company, and who was betrothed to Miss Susan Hart, a celebrated belle of Kentucky, was the Lieutenant-Colonel chosen to aid Bledsoe in these military operations. Colonel Ferguson of the British army was at that time giving the settlement great trouble, sweeping the country near the frontier, gathering in all the loyalists under his standard. When the troops went out against the British under Colonel Ferguson, it was necessary that one of the colonial officers remain behind to protect the inhabitants against the Indians, and as Shelby had no family, he was chosen to lead the forces, and Bledsoe to remain and protect the people against the Indians. Shelby took command of the gallant mountaineers, and gave battle at King's Mountain, on the 7th of October, 1780, considered one of the greatest victories of the frontier army. Colonel Bledsoe, with his brother and kinsman, was almost incessantly engaged with the

Indians in his laborious efforts to subdue the forests and convert the wilds into fields of plenty. Mary Bledsoe, the Colonel's wife, was a remarkable woman, filled with knowledge and noted for independence of thought and action, of remarkable courage and never hesitating to expose herself to the greatest dangers. At the close of 1779, Colonel Bledsoe and his brothers crossed the Cumberland mountains and were so delighted with the beautiful country and the delightful climate that, on their return, they induced their friends and neighbors, of east Tennessee, to seek new homes in the Cumberland Valley. Although Colonel Bledsoe did not remove his own family there for three years, he was the originator of the first expedition which established the first colony in that part of the country. The labors of Colonel Bledsoe and his brother were indefatigable in protecting this little colony, and Mrs. Bledsoe was always a constant and able assistant to her husband. On the night of the 20th of July, 1788, their home was attacked by Indians, and Colonel Anthony Bledsoe was killed. This sad loss was followed by the death of both of her sons at the hands of the Indians, her brother-in-law, a cousin, as well as many friends and earnest supporters of her husband in his work. Bereft of every male relative, almost, and her devoted friends, Mrs. Bledsoe was obliged to undertake the care and education of her little family and the charge of her husband's estate. Her mind was one of almost masculine strength, and she discharged these duties with remarkable ability. Her death came in 1808, but her life of privation, hardship, and Christian courage has placed her among the pioneer mothers and distinguished women of America.

CATHERINE SEVIER

Among the pioneers from the banks of the Yadkin in North Carolina who crossed the mountains to seek new homes in the valley of the Holston, was Samuel Sherrill with his family consisting of several sons and two daughters. One of these daughters, Susan, married Colonel Taylor; the other, Catherine became the second wife of General Sevier. With the family of Sherrill came that of Jacob Brown, from North Carolina. These two families were intimately associated, and intermarried later. Colonel Sherrill took an active part with the Bledsoes against the Cherokee Indians, in 1776. In the attack on the fort, one of the men seeking shelter was killed. A story is told of Miss Sherrill, who was distinguished for her nerve and fleetness of foot. When scrambling over the stockade in her effort to gain an entrance to the fort, she found she was being assisted by some one on the other side. The savages were gaining so rapidly and were then so close upon her that she decided she must leap the wall or die. In leaping over, she fell into the hands of her rescuer, Captain John Sevier. This was their introduction. At this time Captain Sevier was a married man, his wife and younger children not having arrived from Virginia. In 1779, his wife died, leaving him ten children, and in 1780, he and Miss Sherrill were married. Not long after their marriage, Colonel Sevier was called to the duty of raising troops to meet the invasion of the interior of North Carolina by the British, and Colonel Sevier took part in the battle of King's Mountain. His brother was killed in this engagement, and one son severely wounded. The second Mrs. Sevier was the mother of eight children—three sons, and five daughters— making a family of eighteen children, to all of whom Mrs. Sevier was equally devoted. The life of her husband was one of incessant action, adventure, and contest, and the history of the Indian wars of east Tennessee and of the settlement of the country, and the organization of the state government, furnish a record of the deeds of his life. Mrs. Sevier's influence was widespread and evenly exerted, and was resultant of good even among the captive Indian prisoners. The Tories gave Colonel Sevier more personal trouble than even the Indians, as they endeavored to confiscate his property, and Mrs. Sevier was frequently obliged to hide her stock of household articles to protect her family against suffering. She is pictured as tall in stature, stately, with piercing blue eyes, raven locks, and firm mouth, of most commanding presence, inspiring respect and admiration. She devoted her entire life to her husband's advancement and career, and the care of her children. Her trust in God and the power of her husband made her decline on all occasions the protection of the nearest fort, and once when urged "to fort," as it was then called, she said: "I would as soon die by the tomahawk and the scalping knife as by famine. I put my trust in that Power who rules the armies of heaven and among the men on the earth. I know my husband has an eye and an arm for the Indians and the Tories who would harm us, and though he is gone often, and for a week at a time, he comes home when I least expect him and always covered with laurels. If God protects him whom duty calls into danger, so will He those who trust in Him and stand at their post. He would stay out if his family forted." This was the spirit of Catherine Sevier. At one time when attacked by the Tories, who demanded her husband's whereabouts in order to hang him to the highest tree in front of his own house, she replied to the man who stood over her with a drawn pistol: "Shoot! shoot! I am not afraid to die, but remember that while there is a Sevier on the earth my blood will not be unavenged." He did not shoot, and the leader of the band said: "Such a woman is too brave to die." And again when they came to rob her smokehouse and carry off all the meat put aside for her family, she took down the gun which her husband always left her in good order, and said: "The one who takes down a piece of meat is a dead man." Her appearance and manner were so unmistakable that she was left unmolested. She was distinguished for her kindness and liberality to the poor; always gentle and loving, but firm and determined when occasion demanded. The mere motion of her hand was enough for her family and servants to understand that her decision was invincible. Her husband was called upon to serve as the Governor of Tennessee and to a seat in the Congress of the United States. These honors were a great gratification and happiness to her, whose belief and trust in the ability and greatness of her husband never diminished one jot or tittle during his entire life. After his death, in 1815, Mrs. Sevier removed to middle Tennessee, and made her home in a most romantic spot on the side of one of the isolated mountains, and here she resided for years alone save for the attendance of two faithful darky servants. The last few years of her life were spent with her son in Alabama, and there she died on the 2nd of October, 1836, aged eighty-two years.

ANNA INNIS

Mrs. Anna Innis was the widow of Hon. Henry Innis, and the mother of Mrs. John J. Crittenton. She died at Frankfort, Kentucky, May 12, 1851. Her early days, like those of most of the women of her time, were spent in the wilderness but in the society of such men as Clarke, Wayne, Shelby, Scott, Boone, Henderson, Logan, Harte, Nicolas, Murray, Allen, Breckenridge and the heroic spirits of the West.

SARAH RICHARDSON

Another of Kentucky's eminent daughters, who was the mother of General Leslie Combs, was connected with some of the best families of the early days, and came of good Quaker stock from Maryland. The residence of Mrs. Combs was near Boonesborough. She endured hardships that the women of those times and localities were called upon to endure with much courage.

CHARLOTTE ROBERTSON

Was the wife of James Robertson, one of the settlers on the Holston River, friend and companion of General Bledsoe. Charlotte Reeves was the second daughter of George Reeves and Mary Jordon, and was born in Northampton County, North Carolina, in January, 1751. Her husband was one of the pioneers who went with Bledsoe to explore the Hudson Valley, and in February, 1780, Mrs. Robertson joined her husband in the new country. This little party consisted of herself and four small children, her brother, William Reeves, Charles Robertson, her husband's brother, her sister-in-law, three little nieces, two white men servants, and a negro woman and child. They were conveyed in two small, frail, flat boats. Captain James Robertson commanded the party traveling by land, driving the cattle and bringing the few belongings of this little expedition. The perils which they encountered and the difficulties which beset them, traveling through an unexplored country, were beyond anything we of the present day can appreciate. When the little band of travelers reached the Ohio River, the ice was just breaking up, the water rising, and everything so discouraging and dangerous to the small boats, that many became so disheartened they bade adieu to their companions, and sought homes in Natchez. The others, led by Mrs. Robertson, and the only two men of the party living, her brother and brother-in-law, lashed the boats together, and Mrs. Johnson, the widowed sister of Captain Robertson, undertook to serve as pilot and manage the steering oar, while Mrs. Robertson and Hagar, the colored servant, worked at the side oars alternately with Reeves and Robertson. By this slow and most laborious process they made their way up the Ohio to the mouth of the Cumberland, and finally reached their destination, landing in April at what is now the site of Nashville. For years after their removal to this new country, they suffered great privations, and were compelled to live most of the time within the shelter of forts, subjected constantly to attacks by the Indians. Two of Mrs. Robertson's sons were killed, and at one time she suffered the horrible experience of seeing brought from the woods the headless body of one of her beloved sons. It is difficult for us to appreciate the nerve-racking danger which these poor settlers endured, when we read that if one went to the spring for a bucket of water, another must stand watch with his ready gun to protect the first from the creeping stealthy Indian hidden in the thicket ready to take off these settlers one by one. How they ever tilled their fields, or raised their crops under such conditions, is little less than a miracle, and what the life of these poor women must have been, when they could not carry on the common duties of domestic life without seeing the stealthy enemy lurking in the bush, is beyond our conception. In 1794, Mrs. Robertson went on horseback into South Carolina, accompanied by her eldest son to bring out her aged parents who had removed to that state with some of their children. Both lived beyond the eightieth year of their lives in peace and comfort in the home of this devoted daughter. Mrs. Robertson was the mother of eleven children, and lived to an advanced age notwithstanding these experiences, which one might think would have shortened her days. Her manners were always modest and unassuming. She was gentle, kind, affectionate, open-hearted and benevolent, of industrious habits and quiet self-denial, an example to all who knew her, and retained her faculties to the close of her life which occurred in her ninety-third year, on June 11, 1843, at Nashville, Tennessee. General Robertson's death occurred in 1814.

JANE BROWN

Jane Gillespie was born in Pennsylvania about the year 1740. Her father was one of the pioneers of North Carolina. Her early life was spent in the county of Guilford, and two of her brothers, Colonel and Major Gillespie, were noted Revolutionary officers.

About the year 1761, Miss Gillespie became the wife of James Brown, a native of Ireland, whose family had settled in Guilford. At the breaking out of the Revolutionary War, her husband gave his services to his country, leaving his wife with a small family of children. During the retreat of General Greene, in 1781, on the Dan and Deep Rivers, Brown acted as pilot and guide for Colonels Lee and Washington, and through his knowledge of the country, contributed not a little to the successful retreat of the American army, by which they were enabled to elude and break the spirit of the army of Cornwallis. For his services, he received from the state of North Carolina land warrants which entitled him to locate large quantities of land in the wilderness of the mountains. His neighbors made him sheriff of the county, and he was rapidly rising in the esteem of his people. Notwithstanding the fact that his future seemed opening up to brighter and higher things, he realized that he could do more for his family by tearing himself away from these prospects, and he set out on his journey to explore the valley of the Cumberland, taking with him his two eldest sons, William and John, and a few friends. He secured land on the Cumberland River below Nashville. In the winter of 1787, he had returned to Guilford to bring his family into this country. At that time there were two routes to the Cumberland Valley—one down the Tennessee River, and one, the land route, a long and tedious one through the Cumberland gap across the head waters of the Cumberland, Greene, and Barren Rivers. The one down the river was much better when accompanied by women and children, and permitted the transportation of goods, but along the banks of the Tennessee there were many villages of the Cherokee and Chickasaw Indians, with marauding parties of Creeks and Shawnees. Having built a boat in the style of a common flat boat very much like the model of Noah's Ark except that it was open at the top, he entered upon this fearful voyage about the 1st of May, 1788, having on board a large amount of goods, suitable for traffic among the Indians, and his little family and friends. The party consisted of Brown, two sons, three hired men, a negro man (seven men in all), Mrs. Brown, three small sons, four small daughters, an aged woman, and two or three negro women, the property of Brown. Brown had mounted a small cannon on the prow of this boat, and I dare say this was the first man-of-war that ever floated down the Tennessee River. They encountered no trouble until they reached the present site of Chattanooga. Here a party of Indians appeared in canoes, led by a white man by the name of John Vaughn. After pretending to be friendly, and thus gaining admission to his boat through the assurance of this man Vaughn that their intentions were of a thoroughly friendly character, they soon began to throw over his goods into the canoes, break open his chest of treasure, and when Brown attempted to prevent this, he was struck down by an Indian, his head almost severed from his body. They were all taken ashore as captives, Vaughn insisting that these marauders would be punished when the chief arrived. Mrs. Brown, her son George, ten years old, and three small daughters were taken possession of by a party of Creek braves, while the Cherokees were deliberating on the fate of the other prisoners. In one short hour, this poor woman was deprived of husband, sons, friends, and liberty, and began her sad journey on foot along the rugged, flinty trails that led to the Creek towns on the Tallapoosa River. At this time there lived a man named Thomas Turnbridge, a French trader married to a woman who had been taken prisoner near Mobile and raised by the Indians. She had married an Indian brave and had a son twenty-two years old. This son desired to present to his mother some bright-eyed boy as a slave, for according to the savage code of the times, each captive became a slave to his captor. This woman's son was one of the marauding party who had seized Brown's boat, and from the first knew the fate of the party. He tried to induce little Joseph Brown to go with him, but the boy would not; but when the boat landed, he took Joseph to his stepfather Turnbridge, who in good English told the boy he lived near and asked him to spend the night with him. This the poor little frightened fellow consented to do, and while on his way out, he heard the rifles of these savage beasts who were murdering his brothers and friends. Later they came to the Turnbridge house, demanding that the boy be relinquished, and when about to surrender him to the fate of his brothers, the old woman, the wife of Turnbridge, begged for his life, and he was saved only later to be scalped. All of his head was shaved and a bunch of feathers tied to the only remaining lock of hair, his ears pierced with rings, his clothes taken off, and he was supposed to be made one of their tribe. His sisters were brought back by a party of Cherokees, and here they were adopted into different families in this same town with Joseph. From them he learned the fate of his mother, his brother George, and sister Elizabeth. War was now going on between the Indians and the people of Cumberland and east Tennessee. Two thousand warriors, principally Cherokees, were laying waste everything before them in east Tennessee. They had stormed Fort Gillespie, torturing men, women and children, and carrying off Mrs. Glass, the sister of Captain Gillespie. In the spring of 1789, an exchange of prisoners was agreed upon, and a talk held with General Sevier, in which it was stipulated that the Cherokees should surrender all white persons within their borders. When this occurred, young Brown was out on a trading trip, and did not return until all the prisoners had gone up to Running Water. On his return, he was sent also to Running Water, but his little sister would not leave her Indian mother, who had treated her kindly, but Brown finally took her forcibly with him. His eldest sister was claimed by a trader, who said he had bought her with his money. Joseph being unable to redeem her, was obliged to leave her behind. At the conference with the Indians, Brown refused to be exchanged unless his sister was brought in by the Indians, the old chief sent for the girl, and she was brought to Running Water, where on the 1st of May, 1789, young Brown and his sisters were once more restored to liberty. Having nothing and being entirely alone, these three young people were sent to relatives in South Carolina until their mother should be released from captivity from the Creeks. Mrs. Brown's experiences were full of horror and agony, a prisoner with a knowledge of her three children captives among the savages, not knowing what their fate was to be. She was driven forward on foot many days and nights over these terrible roads and through this wild country, arriving at the town of her captors to find herself their slave doomed to work for a savage mistress, and, to add to her distress, her little son and daughter were taken to different towns and she was left alone. At this time Alexander McGillivray, a half-breed Creek of Scotch descent, was chief of the Muscogee Indians, and assumed the title of commander-in-chief of the upper and lower Creeks and the Seminoles, being also the recognized military leader and civil governor of all the Indians of Florida, Alabama and lower Georgia. He combined the shrewdness of the savage with the learning of the civilized man. Mrs. Brown fortunately was taken to a town in which lived the sister of McGillivray, who was the wife of a French trader by the name of Durant. She pitied Mrs. Brown, and told her her brother, the chief of the Creeks, did not approve of his people making slaves of white women, and advised Mrs. Brown to go to him. She offered her a horse and saddle, but told her that she must take them herself. Mrs. Brown being ignorant of the country, an aged Indian was chosen to act as her guide. At an appointed hour, Mrs. Brown mounted her friend's horse, and started in pursuit of her Indian guide, whose demeanor was that of entire ignorance of her existence. As Mrs. Durant had told Mrs. Brown, her brother showed the kindest interest in her story and offered her every protection under his roof. In a few days her savage master appeared and demanded her return. Colonel McGillivray informed him she was in his house and he would protect her. He threatened to kill Mrs. Brown, but McGillivray persuaded him that a dead woman could do no work, and finally offered a rifle, powder and lead, some beads and paint for his wife, which overcame his spirit of revenge, and Mrs. Brown became the ransomed captive of McGillivray. This is a noted instance of the chivalry of the savage chieftain. Here Mrs. Brown taught the Indian women needlework, and they became very fond of her. On a trip to one of the upper Creek towns, McGillivray found Mrs. Brown's daughter, aged eleven years, and purchased her from her master, restoring her to her mother. He also tried to gain possession of her son George, but the Indian who had possession of him had grown very fond of him, and would not surrender him. In November, 1789, Colonel McGillivray arranged for a peace conference at Rock Landing, Georgia, and took Mrs. Brown and her daughter with him and there delivered her to her son William, who had come hoping to hear news of her. After spending some time in South Carolina, she returned to Guilford, at the end of two years only, she had had all these privations and experiences. In 1788, her benefactor, the Creek chieftain, passed through Guilford and paid her a visit. Her brothers offered to pay him any sum for the ransom of Mrs. Brown and the children, but he refused it, and promised to use every effort to restore her son to her. In 1792, a formidable body of Indians, Creeks, Seminoles, and Shawnees invaded the Cumberland Valley, attacking Buchanan Station. Joseph went to the assistance of Buchanan, but the Indians had retreated. What was his astonishment on approaching the scene of action to find his Indian brother lying cold in death. Later on Joseph Brown led a successful campaign against the Indians. His knowledge of the country during his captivity, and the fact that this Indian chieftain had been killed previously, made him well fitted for the position of leader. As they had spared his life, so he spared the lives of the Indian prisoners; and soon after this generous act on his part, his brother, young George Brown, was liberated by the Creeks. In 1812, during the Creek War, a large number of Cherokee Indians offered their services to General Jackson. General Jackson asked Joseph Brown to take command of these Indians, but this he never did. He served as an aid of General

Robards in the army, and was a most valuable interpreter and guide. When General Jackson became President, Colonel Brown obtained an allowance from Congress for a part of the property lost by his father in 1788. Mrs. Brown lived to be ninety years of age, having spent one of the most eventful lives, and exhibited the greatest heroism amidst the trials of the women of even that day. Her son George became a noted citizen of Mississippi, and her captive daughter Jane, the wife of Mr. Collinsworth, became well known in Texas where they resided. No history can do adequate justice to the sufferings and heroism of Mrs. Brown and these early pioneers of the Holston and Cumberland Valleys.

ELIZABETH KENTON

The name of Simon Kenton, one of the early pioneers of Kentucky, is intimately associated with that of Daniel Boone, he being one of the hardy explorers who went into the wilderness of the Alleghany Mountains and spent three years in the wilds near the Kanawha River, until the breaking out of the wars between the Indians and the settlers in 1774, when he tendered his service to his country and acted as a spy. He was captured by the Indians, carried off and the details of his capture form one of the most thrilling stories of these days. He was tied on the back of an unbroken horse and eight times was exposed to what the Indians call "the running of the gauntlet," which consists in giving a man this one chance for his life. He is allowed to run a certain distance, and if he reaches the enclosure selected by the Indians in safety, when all the Indians are shooting at him, he is given his life. He was three times bound to a stake with no prospect of rescue, but suddenly saved through the interference of a friendly-Indian. He was at another time saved through the intercession of Logan, the great Mingo chief, and such experiences filled his almost daily life among his savage captors. He afterwards rendered distinguished service under General

George Rogers Clark and in the campaign of Wayne. General Kenton's first wife was Martha Dowdon, who lived ten years. Elizabeth, his second wife, was the daughter of Stephen Jarboe, a French settler from Maryland, who had come to Mason County, Kentucky, about 1796, when Elizabeth was about seventeen years of age. A clever story is told of the wooing of Elizabeth Jarboe by General Kenton. She had many admirers, among them young Mr. Reuben Clark, and the race seemed close between young Clark and General Kenton; but the wily hero of so many more perilous experiences cleverly outwitted his young friend Clark by sending him on some important work to Virginia, and in his absence General Kenton secured the prize. They were married in the year 1798 at Kenton's Station. A few months after their marriage they removed to Cincinnati, and later to what was then called the Mad River Country, a few miles north of Springfield, Ohio. Here they had many experiences of a thrilling nature with the Indians. General Kenton's family consisted of five children. He was greatly beloved and had most successful influence with the Indians. His home became the rendezvous of both settlers and Indians, which necessitated incessant toil and privation on the part of Mrs. Kenton. General Kenton had lost a great deal of land in Kentucky through the dishonesty of agents whom he had entrusted with his business, and in 1818 they procured only a small portion of some wild land in Logan County, and again took up their residence in Kentucky. In 1836 General Kenton died. In 1842 Mrs. Kenton returned to Indiana and on November 27 passed away. Her daughter was a Mrs. Parkinson of Dayton, who remembers seeing her mother instruct the Indian wife of Isaac Zain.

SARAH WILSON

One of the pioneers to remove to the Cumberland Valley was Joseph Wilson, and he, like the others, suffered great hardships and exposure. In the attack made by the Indians on the 26th of June, 1792, upon the blockhouse erected by the settlers, Mrs. Wilson showed her great courage in insisting that her husband should attempt to escape and seek aid from the other settlers, and that he should leave her and her young children, believing the savages would spare them rather than his life. The blockhouse had been set on fire and there were but a few moments left for his escape. He and his son, a young lad of sixteen years, made a rush through the line of their assailants, but Wilson received a wound in his foot which made it impossible for him to go on for relief, and his son went on hoping to obtain a horse from some neighbor. Immediately on the disappearance of her husband, Mrs. Wilson, with her baby in her arms and followed by five small children, walked slowly out of the fort. Her courage made such an impression upon the Indians that the lives of herself and children were spared. All the rest of the inmates of the fort were killed. Young Wilson obtained relief and carried his father to Bledsoe Station. A party of soldiers hastened to the relief of Mrs. Wilson, but she and her children had been carried off as captives into the Upper Creek Nation. Through the efforts of Colonel White, Mrs. Wilson's brother, after twelve months of captivity, she and her family were restored to their homes. One young girl, however, still remained a captive among the Creeks and it was some time later before she was returned to her own people. She had entirely forgotten her own language and every member of her home circle.

SARAH THORPE

Sarah Thorpe was the wife of Joel Thorpe. They removed from North Haven to Ashtabula County, Ohio, in 1799. An incident is related in the life of Mrs. Thorpe which illustrates the extreme privations to which these early settlers were frequently reduced. In the absence of Mr. Thorpe, who had gone over into

Pennsylvania to procure provisions for his family, it is told that Mrs. Thorpe emptied the straw out of her bed to pick it over to obtain what little wheat there was left in it, and this she boiled and gave to her children. Mrs. Thorpe was married three times. Her first husband was killed in the War of 1812, and her last husband's name was Gardner. The first surveying party to enter the Western Reserve arrived on the Fourth of July, 1796. Permanent settlers did not come in until two years later. In 1708 small settlements were found all over the reserve and a little schooner had been built to ply on the waters of Lake Erie. The necessity for the building of a grist mill near the site of what is now the city of Cleveland is believed to be the foundation of that city. The child of Mr. Kingsberry is believed to be the first white child born in the Western Reserve. The wife of Hon. John Walworth was quite noted among these early settlers. In 1801, it is said, the first ball was given at Cleveland in the log cabin of Major Carter, and here Anna Spofford opened the first school. Mrs. Carter was one of the prominent women of this settlement.

ELIZABETH TAPPEN

Was the second daughter of Alexander and Elizabeth Harper, and was born February 24, 1784, in Harpersfield, New York. She was fifteen years of age when her parents removed to Ohio, and later became one of the teachers in the school which was opened in the Western Reserve. In 1803, Abraham Tappen was appointed to take charge of this school, and alternately he and Miss Harper taught, which was the beginning of their friendship and resulted in their marriage in 1806. Tappen was employed later as a surveyor and took part in the equalizing of the claims of landholders. They became prominent citizens and Mr. Tappen afterwards became a judge. The little village of Unionville is believed to be built on the site of their first home.

REBECCA HEALD

The life of this woman is associated with one of the most prominent incidents and horrible scenes of the War of 1812, the massacre at Fort Dearborn, Chicago. Rebecca Heald was the daughter of Captain Wells of Kentucky. In her early life she resided with her uncle, Captain William Wells, whose life was one of the most singular and romantic of the early border days. He was captured by the Miami Indians when but a very small child, and was adopted by the son of Little Turtle, one of the most famous Indian warriors of the day. After living and becoming completely identified with the lives of his captors, he saw and realized the superior power of the white settlers then fast filling up that section of the country, and he determined to leave his adopted friends and return to his own people, which he did without severing the bonds of friendship then existing. He joined the army of General Wayne, and his services were most conspicuous and valuable through his knowledge of the country and the Indian character. He commanded an organization of spies and fought in the campaign of Wayne until the treaty of Greenville in 1795, which restored peace between the whites and the Indians, when Wells again rejoined his old friends and foster-father, Little Turtle. Captain Wells was chosen to escort the troops from Chicago to Fort Wayne at the time of the outbreak in 1812, and while living there with her uncle, Miss Wells met Captain Heald, and in 1812 Captain Heald was placed in command of the garrison at Chicago, at that time a remote outpost of the American frontier. The communication between the posts at Fort Wayne, Detroit, and Chicago was carried on over an Indian trail with a friendly savage as guide frequently. Opposite the fort which stood at the junction of the Chicago River with Lake Michigan and separated by the river stood the home of Mr. Kinsey. They were the first to have knowledge of the outbreak, which occurred on the night of the 7th of April, 1812. The commander of the fort, Captain Heald, received, on the 7th of August, dispatches from General Hull at Detroit, announcing the declaration of war between the United States and Great Britain. Captain Heald decided upon a plan of action which brought forth the greatest indignation and resentment from his officers and men. He had received orders to distribute all the supplies of United States property equally among the Indians in the neighborhood, and evacuate the post. The officers and men urged upon him the necessity to remain and fortify themselves as strongly as possible, hoping for aid from the other side of the peninsula, but Captain Heald announced that he was going to carry out what seemed to them a foolhardy decision on his part and distribute the property among the Indians and ask them to escort the garrison to Fort Wayne, with the promise of reward for the safe conduct of all, adding that he felt a profound confidence in the profession of friendship on the part of the Indians. This brought on a most unhappy condition of affairs. The troops became almost mutinous, and the Indians set in defiance the restraint which had heretofore been maintained over them. A council with the Indians was held on the 12th of August, none of the officers attending from the fort but Captain Heald. Secret information had been brought that the Indians intended falling upon the officers and murdering them all. Among the chiefs were several who held personal regard for many of the officers and troops in the garrison, and did their utmost to allay the war-like feeling, which was constantly arising and increasing each day among the Indians. On the evening following the last council Black Partridge, a prominent chief, came to the quarters of Captain Heald and said: "Father, I come to deliver up to you the medal I wear. It was given me by the Americans and I have long worn it in token of our mutual friendship, but our young men are resolved to imbrue their hands in the blood of the whites. I cannot restrain them and I will not wear a token of peace while I am compelled to act as an enemy." This should have been enough to allow Captain Heald to appreciate the seriousness of the temper of the Indians, but he went on with his preparation for departure, which was to take place on the 15th. Everyone was ready, reduced to the smallest equipment possible in view of the journey before them. Mr. Kinsey had offered to accompany the troops, intrusting his family to the care of some friendly Indians who had promised to carry them in a boat around the head of Lake Michigan to a place on the St. Joseph River, where they should be joined if the march proved successful. The following morning Mr. Kinsey received word from the chief of St. Joseph's Band that they must expect trouble from the Pottawattamies, urging him to give up his plan to accompany the troops and promising that the boat would be permitted to pass in safety to St. Joseph's, and urged him to go with his family instead, but Mr. Kinsey declined this, believing he might have some influence in restraining the savages. When they reached the point between the prairie and the beach the Pottawattamies took the prairie instead of the beach with the Americans and their purpose was soon evident. They attacked the whites, being about five hundred strong. This little band was soon reduced to about one-third of their number and finally Captain Wells was obliged to surrender, under the agreement that their lives should be spared, and that all should be delivered at one of the British posts to be ransomed later by their friends. Mrs. Heald took an active part in this fight, and through her heroic conduct her life was spared by one of the Indians, who placed her and Mrs. Kinsey and their children in a boat where they were covered with buffalo robes, their rescuer telling the Indians that it contained only the family of Shawneaukee. They were taken back to the home of Mr. Kinsey, closely guarded by the Indians who intended later to take them all to Detroit. After the work of plunder and destruction was complete on the part of the Indians, the fort was set afire. Black Partridge and Wabansee with three others constituted themselves protectors to the family of Mr. Kinsey. Mrs. Heald and Mrs. Kinsey later succeeded in disguising themselves as French women with some of the clothes they found in the house, and were conducted by Black Partridge to the home of Ouilmette, a Frenchman with a half-breed wife, who had been employed by Mr. Kinsey and whose home was near. Only the absolute devotion on the part of Black Partridge saved these women from massacre. Later they were successfully placed in a boat, and under the care of a half-breed interpreter were taken to St. Joseph and later to Detroit under the escort of Chandonnai, a faithful Indian friend, and the entire party with their servants delivered up as prisoners of war to the British commanding officer. General Hull at the surrender of Detroit had stipulated that all American inhabitants should remain undisturbed in their homes, and here Mrs. Kinsey and Mrs. Heald were allowed to peacefully reside. Mr. Kinsey, through anxiety for his family, ultimately joined them and surrendered as a prisoner of war. During the fight of which we have spoken Mrs. Heald received seven wounds. Lieutenant Helm was taken by some friendly Indians to their village of the Au Sable, and then to St. Louis, where he was ultimately liberated. Mrs. Helm accompanied her father's family to Detroit. During the engagement, she had a horse shot from under her. The little remnant of the garrison at Fort Dearborn with their wives and children were distributed among the villages of the Pottawattamies upon the Illinois, Wabash, Rock River and Milwaukee until the spring, when they were taken to Detroit and ransomed. Mrs. Helm, spoken of, was the daughter of Captain Killip, a British officer attached to one of the companies, who in 1794 aided the Indian tribes against the United States Government. On the death of her husband, Colonel Killip, she afterward became the wife of John Kinsey and removed to Chicago, there establishing a thriving trading post among the Pottawattamie Indians. Their daughter married Lieutenant Lina J. Helm, of Kentucky, and is the one spoken of in this account.

ABIGAIL SNELLING

Was the daughter of Thomas Hunt, a Revolutionary officer and a native of Watertown, Massachusetts. Her father had entered the American army as a volunteer, but soon received his commission as a regular officer and was in the expedition against Ticonderoga, commanded by Ethan Allen, one of the small band who made themselves masters of Crown Point. He was with General Wayne at Stony Point, and in 1794 went with him in the campaign against the Indians. In 1798, he received the promotion to Lieutenant-Colonel, First Regiment Infantry, and was placed in command of Fort Wayne, remaining until the death of Hantramack at Detroit, when Lieutenant-Colonel Hunt succeeded to the command and became the colonel of the regiment and in command of the post at Detroit, afterwards succeeding to that at Mackinaw. Abigail Hunt was but six weeks old when the family arrived at Mackinaw. When she was but seven years of age, her parents left Mackinaw on their way to St. Louis by way of Detroit. On their journey they stopped for a short time at Fort Wayne, where Colonel Hunt's eldest daughter was married to the surgeon of the post, Dr. Edwards. Colonel Hunt took command of the garrison at the mouth of the Missouri, eighteen miles above St. Louis. This was about the time of the Burr conspiracy, and a court-martial was held there to try Major BrufT, who was supposed to be a party to the conspiracy, but who was acquitted. Lewis and Clark arrived at this post from their exploring expedition, causing the greatest excitement and curiosity owing to their costumes made entirely of skins and furs. The captain in one of the companies of Colonel Hunt's regiment at that time was a man by the name of Pike, who afterwards became famous as General Pike, and was selected by the government to explore the upper Mississippi, being absent on this expedition almost two years. In 1809 Colonel Hunt died, and six months later followed the death of Mrs. Hunt. The eldest son resided in Detroit, and after the death of his mother, he removed the family to Waltham, Massachusetts, to reside with their maternal grandfather, Samuel Wellington. This brother later became Colonel Henry J. Hunt. When the War of 1812 was declared, no one among the officers then in the service was more distinguished than one Captain Snelling. When General Hull arrived with his army at Detroit early in July, Dr. Edwards, who had married Colonel Hunt's eldest daughter, joined General Hunt's army at Dayton, and with him was John E. Hunt, so that the sisters were again brought together. Here Captain Snelling was introduced to Miss Hunt by Major Edwards, and in a very short time they were engaged. On the 13th of August, Miss Hunt was married to Captain Snelling by a chaplain in General Hull's army. Captain Snelling had quite distinguished himself in the fight at Brownstown under General Hull. Three days after their marriage, the British landed at Springwells and Captain Snelling with others was humiliated by having General Hull retire before the enemy, and it is reported that when an aid asked Captain Snelling to help him plant the white flag, he replied with indignation: "No, sir, I will not soil my hands with that flag." General Hull was so panic-stricken that he surrendered the fortress without even demanding terms, and words cannot express the disgust and indignation of these brave soldiers as they stacked their arms to be taken over by the British. Colonel Hunt was permitted to remain in Detroit as a prisoner, accompanied by John Hunt, but Captain Snelling and his family were placed on board a boat which was to convey General Hull and his command as prisoners of war to Erie, where they were turned over to the British guards. Mrs. Snelling and the women were taken care of by the captain of the boat with promises that they should rejoin their husbands at Fort George, but it was some time before they were reunited. One of the strange incidents of war was that a British officer who had been most cruel and unkind to Captain Snelling, whose courteous treatment in contrast to that which he had received, so embarrassed and humiliated him that he apologized, and they became fast friends. Captain Snelling was one of the most unbending patriots, and at one time when the troops were in Montreal, the order was given for hats off in front of Nelson's monument, the guard knocking off the hats of the prisoners, but on an officer attempting such with Captain Snelling he received the quick warning, "At your peril, sir, touch me." Later he received the apology of the officer in question. The married officers were soon paroled and sent to Boston, where Captain Snelling and his wife remained until he was ordered to Plattsburg to join General Hampton's army. Their eldest child, Mary, was born when Mrs. Snelling was but sixteen years of age. Captain Snelling rapidly rose in distinction, and was on the staff of General Izard as Inspector-General, stationed at Buffalo. On peace being declared Snelling was made Lieutenant-Colonel of the Sixth Infantry and ordered to Governor's Island, and later to Plattsburgh, where he remained four years, when the order came to start for the upper Mississippi by way of St. Louis. Their family then consisted of Mrs. Snelling and three children, her youngest sister, and one brother, a graduate from West Point, Lieutenant Wellington Hunt, also a married man. Mrs. Snelling's sister, Eliza N. Hunt, married a man by the name of Soulard, a French gentleman.

The following summer, Snelling received his colonelcy and was placed in command of the Fifth Regiment and ordered to relieve Lieutenant-Colonel Leavenworth, who had been promoted to another regiment, and Captain Snelling conducted his regiment to within eight miles of the Falls of St. Anthony, where Fort Snelling, Minnesota, now stands. Enroute he held councils with the Indians of Prairie Little Du Chien, where he found Governor Cass. Their first occupation in their new home was the building of the log barracks and fort which were to form the homes and protection of the regiment and its officers. These rude quarters were papered and carpeted with buffalo robes and here Mrs. Snelling's fifth child was born. It was a two years' struggle before the post was completed. In June, 1823, the first steamboat made its appearance on the upper Mississippi, and caused great excitement among the troops. A French gentleman brought letters of introduction to Mrs. Snelling from friends in St. Louis, being invited by the Colonel to remain as long as it was his pleasure. He found it most agreeable, as Mrs. Snelling spoke French fluently. At one time this post was visited by General Scott, and he ordered the name of Fort St. Anthony, which it then bore, changed to Fort Snelling in approval of Colonel Snelling's labors. In 1825 the family left Fort Snelling and visited Mrs. Snelling's brother, Lieutenant Wellington Hunt, in command at Detroit. In 1826 Captain Thomas Hunt, then residing at Washington, wrote his sister to send her two eldest children to him to be educated, and her eldest daughter, Mary, was sent with Captain and Mrs. Plympton who were going to that city. In 1827, the regiment was ordered to Jefferson Barracks, St. Louis, and during the winter Colonel Snelling went on to Washington on business, and was there when his daughter Mary died, the effects of a cold taken at a ball. As Colonel Snelling was obliged to remain in Washington for some time, Mrs. Snelling with her three children joined him there, and a few months after her arrival Colonel Snelling died. After his death she lived on her farm near Detroit, later removing into the city. In 1841, Mrs. Snelling married Rev. J. E. Chaplain, the grandson of President Edwards, who was appointed principal of one of the branches in the Michigan State Institution. Mrs. Chaplain's son, James Snelling, was with General Worth and took part in the battle of Palo Alto, and other battles under General Taylor.

The later years of Mrs. Chaplain's life were spent with her daughter, Mrs. Hazard, in Cincinnati.

MARY MCMILLAN

There were but a few small settlements along the Lakes, and in 1688 Sault Ste. Marie was one of the most prominent French posts and a favorite resort for traders. Michigan had passed from the possession of the French to Great Britain in 1760. The military occupation taking place at the time of the Pontiac war extends through the struggles of the British, Indians and Americans to obtain possession of the country down to the victory of Commodore Perry. Then comes the opening up of the country, followed by the period of agriculture, manufacturing and commerce of to-day. The early French were engaged in the fur trading business, and, under the control of the British, they were allowed to pursue this occupation. During the Revolutionary troubles the peninsula remained in quiet, and the treaty in 1783 included it in the bounds of American territory, and in 1795, after the victories of General Wayne, settlers began to go in and open up the country. In 1810 Mackinaw was the chief trading point. Among these early settlers of the eastern portion of Michigan was Mary McMillan, who with her husband had removed to this new land. In 1813, Mr. McMillan had left his family to take part in the military operations of that time, leaving Mrs. McMillan alone to care for her little family. One day while away from home to secure food, she became nervous over the fate which might have overtaken her little ones in her absence, which anxiety was not ill founded, as they had all disappeared with the entire contents of her house. Being of a courageous nature, she was undaunted by the realization of her fears and followed the Indians to find her children hid in the woods on the opposite side of the river.

She suffered many like experiences of terror and anxiety during the absence of her husband. After the war was over, when they were living near Detroit, Mr. McMillan was murdered by Indians and her son, eleven years old, captured. After four months' absence, she obtained the news of his whereabouts and raised the money necessary for his ransom, when he was restored to his mother.

CHARLOTTE CLARK

Her husband was a commissary officer with the troops who were with Colonel Leavenworth on the upper Mississippi. The daughter of Mrs. Clark was Mrs. Van Cleve of Ann Arbor, Michigan, and was born while the troops were stationed at Prairie Du Chien. They later resided at Fort Snelling. Mrs. Clark was described as a very handsome woman with unusual intelligence and great charm in conversation. Her son, Malcolm Clark, was a trader among the Indians near Fort Benton in Oregon, and married one of the women of the Black Foot Tribe. His two daughters were educated at Ann Arbor. One of Mrs. Clark's daughters, Charlotte Clark, was Mrs. Gear, the wife of Hezekiah Gear, one of the early pioneers of Illinois, and resided at Galena.

SARAH BRYAN

Was conspicuous among the early settlers of Michigan as the wife of John Bryan.

SYLVIA CHAPIN

The wife of Syrena Chapin was considered one of the oldest settlers and pioneers of Buffalo, where Dr. Chapin came with his family in 1805. Her husband was a man very much beloved by the citizens of Buffalo.

MRS. ANDERSON

One of the early settlers of Plymouth, Wayne County, Michigan.

ELIZA BULL

Eliza Bull, afterwards Mrs. Sinclair, was also an early pioneer of Michigan.

MARY ANN RUMSEY

One of the early residents of Ann Arbor, Michigan, the county seat of Washtenaw County. This Indian name signified grand or beautiful, and the Grand River takes its name from this word. The name Ann Arbor was given to this little village by John Allen and Walter Rumsey who came to the settlement in February, 1824, from New York State. Mary Ann Rumsey, the wife of Walter Rumsey, was quite a remarkable character and many interesting stories are told of her own life in these early days. Mr. Rumsey died at Ann Arbor, and his wife afterwards married Mr. Van Fossen, and removed to Indiana.

There was another woman who bore the name of Ann quite distinguished in this little settlement to which she came in 1824 with the parents of her husband, James Turner Allen, from Virginia. The local tradition is that to these two women, Ann Allen and Ann Rumsey, the town of Ann Arbor is indebted for the addition of Ann to its name. After the death of Mr. Allen his widow returned to Virginia. Mrs. Allen's maiden name was Barry. Her husband's name was Dr. McCue, a Virginian.

BETTY O'FLANAGAN

Among the remarkable characters of the early days of Detroit there is mention made of one very unique person, Betty O'Flanagan, who is said to have been one of the followers of Wayne's army. When listening to her reminiscences she often told the young people that she would have been better off had "Mad Anthony" lived.

HARRIET L. NOBLE

Quite a wave of excitement spread over western New York in 1824, over the opportunities offered in the new country known as Michigan. Among those seized with the mania was Nathaniel Noble, and in January of that year he with his brother and family set out for their new home, joining in Ann Arbor their former friends, John Allen and Walter Rumsey. The deprivations and hardships of the journey are only a repetition of those which we have already given. The town of Dixborough was laid out by Mr. Dix of Massachusetts. Miss Frances Trask was a cousin of Mrs. Dix, and was one of the remarkable characters of this day. She was a noted belle and coquette of the community, possessing fine qualities of heart and real worth ; her eccentricities and unfeminine defiance of general opinion often caused great talk and comment among her neighbors. She was a general favorite owing to her wit, force, and happy disposition, among the men and many amusing stories are told of her ready repartee. She was at one time engaged to Sherman Dix, a relative of her brother-in-law, but married a Mr. Thompson, being left quite early a widow. Her nephew by marriage was at one time the Secretary of State in Texas.

MRS. HECTOR SCOTT

Mrs. Hector Scott is worthy of mention among the early settlers of Michigan. She was the daughter of Luther Martin, the attorney who so successfully defended Aaron Burr. One of the famous beauties of that time was a Mrs. Talbot, who was the daughter of Commodore Truxton.

MRS. MOSELEY

Mrs. Moseley is also deserving of mention. She was the daughter of the Missionary Bingham, and was said to be the first white child born in the Sandwich Islands.

REBECCA J. FISHER

Mrs. Fisher gives the following facts regarding her life and harrowing experiences as a daughter of pioneer parents:

"I was born in Philadelphia, Pennsylvania, August 31, 1831, and came to Texas with my parents, Johnstone and Mary Gilleland, and two little brothers, about 1836 or 1837. My father was one of the bravest, most conscientious and active soldiers of the Republic of Texas, and had come home for a few days to look after his family when a cruel death awaited him.

"The day my parents were murdered was one of those days which youth and old age so much enjoy. It was in strange contrast to the tragedy at its close. We were only a few rods from the house. Suddenly the war whoop of the Comanche burst upon our ears, sending terror to all hearts. My father, in trying to reach the house for weapons, was shot down, and near him my mother, clinging to her children and praying God to spare them, was also murdered. As she pressed us to her heart we were baptized in her precious blood. We were torn from her

86

dying embrace and hurried off into captivity, the chiefs wife dragging me to her horse and clinging to me with a tenacious grip. She was at first savage and vicious looking, but from some cause her wicked nature soon relaxed, and folding me in her arms, she gently smoothed back my hair, indicating that she was very proud of her suffering victim. A white man with all the cruel instincts of the savage was with them. Several times they threatened to cut off our hands and feet if we did not stop crying. Then the woman, in savage tones and gestures, would scold, and they would cease their cruel threats. We were captured just as the sun was setting and were rescued the next morning.

"During the few hours we were their prisoners, the Indians never stopped. Slowly and stealthily they pushed their way through the settlement to avoid detection, and just as they halted for the first time the soldiers suddenly came upon them, and firing commenced. As the battle raged, the Indians were forced to take flight. Thereupon they pierced my little brother through the body, and, striking me with some sharp instrument on the side of the head, they left us for dead, but we soon recovered sufficiently to find ourselves alone in that dark, dense forest, wounded and covered with blood.

"Having been taught to ask God for all things, we prayed to our Heavenly Father to take care of us and direct us out of that lonely place. I lifted my wounded brother, so faint and weak, and we soon came to the edge of a large prairie, when as far away as our swimming eyes could see we discovered a company of horsemen. Supposing them to be Indians, frightened beyond expression, and trembling under my heavy burden, I rushed back with him into the woods and hid behind some thick brush. But those brave men, on the alert, dashing from place to place, at last discovered us. Soon we heard the clatter of horses' hoofs and the voices of our rescuers calling us by name, assuring us they were our friends who had come to take care of us. Lifting the almost unconscious little sufferer, I carried him out to them as best I could. With all the tenderness of women, their eyes suffused with tears, those good men raised us to their saddles and hurried ofT to camp, where we received every attention and kindness that man could bestow.

"I was seven years of age when my parents were murdered. Over seventy years have passed since then, and yet my heart grows faint as that awful time passes in review. It is indelibly stamped upon memory's pages and photographed so deeply upon my heart that time with all its changes can never erase it."

In 1848 Rebecca J. Gilleland married Rev. Orceneth Fisher, D.D., a prominent and distinguished minister of the Methodist Church. For over sixty years they served the church in Texas and California, organizing it in Oregon. Dr. Fisher died in Austin, Texas, some years ago. Mrs. Fisher has been president of many church associations, was Acting President of the Daughters of the Republic of Texas for twelve years, and is even yet in the evening of a long and honored life, surrounded by children, grandchildren and great-grandchildren, the distinguished member or guest of many patriotic clubs and societies.

EARLY SETTLERS

The Pacific Coast Company was founded by John Jacob Astor, of New York, in 1810, to carry on trading operations on the Pacific Coast. These exploring parties started from Astoria, Oregon, and experienced the greatest privations and hardships in these trips, the Indians of that time being most hostile and determined in their opposition against the approach of white settlers. The war between Great Britain and the United States breaking out, the Hudson Bay Company took possession of Astoria, and in 1812 a party of traders under the command of Mr. Reed, accompanied by Pierre Dorian, an interpreter, with his wife and two children started on a expedition into the "Snake Country." For almost a year nothing was heard of this little party, until the following summer, when they arrived at Walla

Walla, and the accounts given of the hardships of this tribe and the heroism of Mrs. Dorian hardly have a parallel.

In the summer of 1846 a band of settlers started for California, and their experiences and adventures fill one of the darkest pages of our early history. The party consisted of J. F. Reed, wife and four children; Jacob Donner, wife and seven children; William Pike, wife and two children; William Foster, wife and one child; Lewis Kiesburg, wife and one child; Mrs. Murphy, a widow, with five children; William McCutcheon, wife and one child; W. H. Eddy, wife and two children; Noah James, Patrick Dolan, Patrick Shoemaker, John Denton, C. F. Stanton, Milton Elliott, Joseph Raynhard, Augustus Spiser, John Baptiste, Charles Burger, Baylis Williams, and a man by the name of Smith, one by the name of Antoin, and one by the name of Herring. They were well supplied with wagons, teams, cattle, provisions, arms, and ammunition. On reaching White Water River, on the eastern side of the Rocky Mountains, they were persuaded by one of their party to take a new route to California. This brought upon them the greatest suffering, ultimate disaster and the annihilation of almost the entire little band. Many animals were lost; those which survived were exhausted and broken down. Many of their own party gave up their lives. Thirty days were occupied in traveling forty miles. They were lost in the desert for some time, being without water and almost all of their supplies exhausted. Attacked by the Indians, they lost several of their ablest defenders and many of their animals. They reached the mountains in the most distressed condition. It was then the fall of the year, late in October. On the evening of the 22nd, they crossed the Truckee River the forty-ninth time in eighty miles, and on October 28th they reached Truckee Lake at the foot of Fremont's Pass of the main chain of the Sierra Nevadas. This pass at this point is 9,838 feet high. After struggling to the top of the pass they found the snow five feet deep. Frequent efforts to cross the mountains proved useless, and they found they would be compelled to winter here. They retraced their steps to a lower level and commenced the erection of cabins. On the 21st of November, it is said, six women and sixteen men made an attempt to cross the mountains for provisions. Many of this little band died of starvation. On the 1 6th of December, another effort was made by a small party on snow-shoes. The records of this little band contain some of the most heartrending stories and revolting details. Cannibalism was forced upon them, and the bodies of many who died were consumed to satisfy those of sterner strength. This camp is known in history as "The Camp of Death." Several men forsook the camp to save their lives and perished of starvation on the mountains. The news of the condition of these emigrants had reached California, and an effort was made on the part of the government to send them relief. Two expeditions failed to cross the mountains, but finally a small party of seven men reached the camp. Fourteen men had died of starvation and others were too weak to even be carried. The annals of human suffering nowhere present a more appalling spectacle than that which greeted the eyes of this little rescuing party. The women seemed to withstand the suffering better even than the men. The names of Mrs. Reed, Mrs. Eddy, Mrs. Pike, are conspicuous for their heroism among those who lived, and among the survivors who ultimately reached California were, Mary Graves, Ellen Graves, Nancy Graves, Viney Graves, Elizabeth Graves, Sarah Fosdick, Georgianna Donner, Elizabeth Donner, Mary Donner, Mrs. Wolfinger, Mrs. Kiesburg, Sarah Foster, Mary Murphy, Harriet Pike, Miriam Pike, Margaret Brinn, Isabell Brinn, Virginia Reed, and Pattie Reed. Throughout the horrible scenes of this disastrous expedition the courage, devotion, and fortitude of the women stand out conspicuously. When the hearts of the stoutest men sank, the unflinching energy of the women was shown. When men became mere brutes, woman's true nobility shone forth and her power of soul over body was proven, and the history of this expedition stands as a memorial to what women may endure and accomplish.

Mrs. Reed's daughter, Mrs. Virginia Reed Murphy, of Springfield, Massachusetts, is very well known. She wrote an interesting account of these experiences of her parents and herself, which appeared in the "Century Magazine."

PIETY LUCRETIA HADLEY

Mrs. Hadley was the daughter of Major David Smith, by his second wife, Obedience Fort Smith, and was born in Logan County, Kentucky, in April 1807. Her early life was spent in Mississippi and Kentucky. On June 14 1831, Miss Smith was married to Mr. T. B. J. Hadley of Jackson, Mississippi. Of this union there were five daughters. In 1840 Colonel and Mrs. Hadley moved to Houston, Texas. She was one of the conspicuous figures of Texas.

MIREBEAN B. LAMAR

Mrs. Lamar was the daughter of a celebrated Methodist minister, John Newland Maffitt, and sister of Fred Maffitt, commodore in the Confederate Navy. She was the wife of the first vice-president and the second president of the republic of Texas, John Lamar, who had come to Texas from Georgia, his native state, in 1835, rendered conspicuous service in the Battle of San Jacinto; was President Burnet's Secretary of War. Immediately after her marriage, Mrs. Lamar and her husband moved to their plantation near the town of Richmond on the Brazos River. In 1857 General Lamar accepted a mission to one of the American Republics, and while on his visit to Washington to receive his credentials, Mrs. Lamar was greatly admired and became one of the belles of the Capital City. While on this visit she was taken seriously ill and returned to their southern home. After two years' service abroad and on General Lamar's return to Texas he was stricken with apoplexy. During the war she did conspicuous service for her people and will long be remembered by the victims of the lost cause. Her death, October 8, 1871, caused unfeigned sorrow.

MRS. JOHN RAGAN

Was Miss Molly Ford Taylor before her marriage and was a conspicuous figure among the prominent women of Texas in 1875. She was with her husband when he took his seat for the third time in the House of Representatives. Her home in Texas was Fort Houston near Palestine and was noted for the graceful hospitalities dispensed by its mistress.

MRS. THOMAS J. RUSK

General Thomas J. Rusk having lost his fortune removed from his native state of South Carolina to Clarksville, Georgia, to practice law. Here he married a daughter of General Cleveland, a prominent man of this section. Forming some business connection, his assistants absconded to Texas with the funds of the corporation and he pursued the fugitives in an attempt to recover the stolen property. This was in 1835, and he followed them as far as Nacogdoches, Texas. Here the whole country was in a state of the wildest excitement. Everything was aflame with the spirit of Revolution. He soon became interested and forgetting everything else took up the cause of the patriots as his own. He joined one of the companies and soon became its commander and from that the leader of the little Republic's undisciplined battalions. He was sent by the people to the memorable convention of 1836 that declared the independence of Texas, and took service under the new government as its first Secretary of War, and as such, stopped Houston's army before Santa Anna and brought on the celebrated Battle of San Jacinto and distinguished himself in this battle so that he has since been considered one of the heroes in the history of Texas. In Houston's administration he was again called into the cabinet, resigning to take a seat in the Texas Congress. He was a conspicuous figure in the Indian warfare against the Caddos and Cherokees and other hostile tribes who gave the settlers at that time so much trouble. When more peaceful conditions prevailed he was appointed chief justice of the Republic, and later resigned and resumed his practice of law. He was in favor of the annexation to the United States and in 1845 was President to the convention which formed the constitution of the then future state of Texas. He was elected to the first legislature and held this position until his death in 1857. General Rusk's career gave Mrs. Rusk a position of great prominence in her State. She filled with great courage and energy all duties which these positions entailed. Their life on this early frontier showed her to be one of the women of which America is proud and to which we owe the opening up of these new countries which are now such great and glorious states of our Union. Mrs. Rusk was the mother of seven children. She died in 1856, in the forty-seventh year of her age.

MRS. SIDNEY SHERMAN

Mrs. Sherman's husband was a lineal descendant of Roger Sherman. Her father was married in 1835 and lived at Newport, Kentucky. The cry of distress from Texas reached the ears of young Captain and Mrs. Sidney Sherman and they felt it their duty to go to its assistance. Captain Sherman raised and equipped a company of fifty men and in 1835 embarked for the scene of his future exploits. Mrs. Sherman accompanied the expedition as far as Natchez, but from there she returned to her parents in Frankfort, Captain Sherman continuing on to Texas and arriving there in February, 1836. He took part in the engagement which preceded and led his regiment in the last stand made by the Texans on the San Jacinto. All through these trying days in the early history of Texas, Colonel Sherman bore a conspicuous part. In 1842 he was elected to Congress from his district, and some years later by popular vote Major-General of the Texan Army, and this he held until Texas was annexed to the United States. Colonel Sherman suffered severe losses prior to the war and during that period. His young son, Lieutenant Sidney Sherman, was killed. This so told upon Mrs. Sherman's health that she died in January, 1865.

LUCY HOLCOMB PICKENS

Mrs. Pickens was one of the famous beauties of Texas. In 1856 she married Colonel Pickens, a member of Congress from South Carolina. In the following year her husband was appointed, by President Buchanan, Minister of the United States to the Imperial court of Russia, and in St. Petersburg she was no less famous as a beauty and remarkably gifted woman than in her own land. In i860 Colonel Pickens resigned his commission, having been elected Governor of South Carolina, and here Mrs. Pickens discharged with inimitable grace and dignity her duties as the wife of the Governor, and it was said that General Pickens on the twelfth day of April, 1861, at Charleston, took his little daughter in his arms and placed in her tiny hand the lighted match that fired the first gun of the war on Fort Sumter. Mrs. Pickens held all through her life the friendship of the Imperial family of Russia, and on the marriage of their daughter, "Doushka", a silver tea service was sent her by the Imperial family. Mrs. Pickens died some years ago.

MRS. ALEXANDER W. TERRELL

Mrs. Terrell's home was in Austin. Her husband was Minister to Turkey at one time and she traveled extensively in Europe. Her attractive personality and strength of character made her, before her recent death, one of the conspicuous figures of the prominent women of Texas.

MRS. WILLIAM H. WHARTON

Was the daughter of Jared E. Groce, who went to Texas in 1821. Their home, Groce's Retreat, on the Brazos River, near the town of Hempstead, is well-known in Texas. Sarah Groce married when quite young William H. Wharton, a brilliant young lawyer, who had gone to Texas from Nashville, Tennessee, in 1829. He was president of the convention in 1833, held to dissolve the bond which united Texas to Mexico, and two years later was in the Texan Army at San Antonio. He was sent to the general consultation of the United States as one of the three commissioners and the following year was accredited to that Government as Minister from the Republic of Texas. Later he was elected to the Senate of the Republic, where he attained distinction. In 1839 his death was the result of an accident. Mrs. Wharton is remembered as one of the most forceful women in the political and social life of Texas, and some of her letters addressed to the prominent public women in the dark days when the prospects of Texan independence was in doubt are filled with a fervor, patriotism and energy worthy of the women in the heroic days of Carthage, and her appeals for the cause of human liberty were not unheeded and she is to-day believed to have been one of the potent powers of that time.

Mrs. Wharton died in the late seventies. She had one son, General John A. Wharton, who served throughout the Civil War in the Confederate Army, but was afterward killed. His only daughter died unmarried, so that no direct descendants survive this pioneer woman.

MISS PETERSON

Among the heroic women of the early days, we find many instances in those who went to California with the settlers. One of these was Miss Peterson, who aided in saving the lives of some miners who were perishing in the mountains of starvation. On being told of their condition by an Indian, she insisted on going to their rescue.

KATE MOORE

There is a very interesting incident told of the bravery of one Kate Moore who resided on one of the islands in the south. She was brought to America by Grace Darling. Many disasters had overtaken vessels landing at Montauk Point, so upon taking up her residence near by she was constantly on the alert. She so trained her ear that she could tell the difference between the howling of the storm and the cries for help, and thus direct a boat, which she herself had learned to manage, in the darkest night to the spot where these poor, perishing mariners could be found. She was a person of fine education and great refinement, but adapted herself to her father's humble calling, and no night was too dark, nor storm too severe for her hand to be ready to launch her boat and aid in the rescue, and in fifteen years she had personally saved the lives of twenty-one persons.

A Chapter from
The Part Taken by Women in American History, 1912

MATRONS AND MAIDENS
WHO CAME IN THE MAYFLOWER

By Annie Russell Marble

It has been said, with some justice, that the Pilgrims were not remarkable men, that they lacked genius or distinctive personalities. The same statement may be made about the women. They did possess, as men and women, fine qualities for the work which they were destined to accomplish,—remarkable energy, faith, purpose, courage and patience. These traits were prominent in the leaders, Carver and Bradford, Standish and Winslow, Brewster and Dr. Fuller. As assistants to the men in the civic life of the colony, there were a few women who influenced the domestic and social affairs of their own and later generations. From chance records, wills, inventories and traditions their individual traits must be discerned, for there is scarcely any sequential, historic record.

Death claimed some of these brave-hearted women before the life at Plymouth really began. Dorothy May Bradford, the daughter of Deacon May of the Leyden church, came from Wisbeach, Cambridge; she was married to William Bradford when she was about sixteen years old and was only twenty when she was drowned at Cape Cod. Her only child, a son, John, was left with her father and mother in Holland and there was long a tradition that she mourned grievously at the separation. This son came later to Plymouth, about 1627, and lived in Marshfield and Norwich, Connecticut.

The tiny pieces of a padded quilt with faded threads of silver and gold, which belonged to Rose Standish[1], are fitting relics of this mystical, delicate wife of "the doughty Captain." She died January 29, 1621. She is portrayed in fiction and poetry as proud of her husband's bravery and his record as a Lieutenant of Queen Elizabeth's forces in aid of the Dutch. She was also proud of his reputed, and disputed, inheritance among the titled families of Standish of Standish and Standish of Duxbury Hall.[2] There has been a persistent tradition that Rose was born or lived on the Isle of Man and was married there, but no records have been found as proofs.

In the painting of "The Embarkation," by Robert Weir, Elizabeth Barker, the young wife of Edward Winslow, is attired in gay colors and extreme fashion, while beside her stands a boy of about eight years with a canteen strapped over his shoulders. It has been stated that this is the silver canteen, marked "E. W.," now in the cabinet of the Massachusetts Historical Society. The only record *there* is[3] "presentation, June, 1870, by James Warren, Senr., of a silver canteen and pewter plate which once belonged to Gov. Edward Winslow with his arms and initials." As Elizabeth Barker, who came from Chatsun or Chester, England, to Holland, was married April 3, 1618, to Winslow,[4] and as she was his first wife, the son must have been a baby when *The Mayflower* sailed. Moreover, there is no record by Bradford of any child that came with the Winslows, except the orphan, Ellen

---

1 Now in Pilgrim Hall, Plymouth.

2 For discussion of the ancestry of Standish, see "Some Recent Investigations of the Ancestry of Capt. Myles Standish," by Thomas Cruddas Porteus of Coppell, Lancashire; N. E. Gen. Hist. Register, 68; 339-370; also in edition, Boston, 1914.

3 Massachusetts Historical Society Proceedings, iv, 322.

4 England and Holland of the Pilgrims, Dexter.

More. It has been suggested that the latter was of noble lineage.[5]

Mary Norris, of Newbury in England, wife of one of the wealthiest and most prominent of the Pilgrims in early years, Isaac Allerton, died in February of the first winter, leaving two young girls, Remember and Mary, and a son, Bartholomew or "Bart." The daughters married well, Remember to Moses Maverick of Salem, and Mary to Thomas Cushman. Mrs. Allerton gave birth to a child that was still-born while on *The Mayflower* and thus she had less strength to endure the hardships which followed.[6]

When Bradford, recording the death of Katherine Carver, called her a "weak woman," he referred to her health which was delicate while she lived at Plymouth and could not withstand the grief and shock of her husband's death in April. She died the next month. She has been called "a gracious woman" in another record of her death.[7] She was the sister or sister-in-law of John Robinson, their pastor in England and Holland. Recent investigation has claimed that she was first married to George Legatt and later to Carver.[8] Two children died and were buried in Holland in 1609 and 1617 and, apparently, these were the only children born to the Carvers. The maid Lois, who came with them on *The Mayflower*, is supposed to have married Francis Eaton, but she did not live after 1622. Desire Minter, who was also of the Carver household, has been the victim of much speculation. Mrs. Jane G. Austin, in her novel, "Standish of Standish," makes her the female scapegrace of the colony, jealous, discontented and quarrelsome. On the other hand, and

5 The Mayflower Descendant, v. 256.

6 History of the Allerton Family; W. S. Allerton, N. Y., 1888.

7 New England Memorial; Morton.

8 The Colonial, I, 46; also Gen. Hist. Reg., 67; 382, note.

still speculatively, she is portrayed as the elder sister and house keeper for John Howland and Elizabeth Tilley, after the death of Mistress Carver; this is assumed because the first girl born to the Howlands was named Desire.[9] The only known facts about Desire Minter are those given by Bradford, "she returned to friends and proved not well, and dyed in England."[10] By research among the Leyden records, collated by H. M. Dexter,[11] the name, Minter, occurs a few times. William Minter, the husband of Sarah, was associated with the Carvers and Chiltons in marriage betrothals. William Minter was purchaser of a house from William Jeppson, in Leyden, in 1614. Another record is of a student at the University of Leyden who lived at the house of John Minter. Another reference to Thomas Minter of Sandwich, Kent, may furnish a clue.[12] Evidently, to some of these relatives, with property, near or distant of kin, Desire Minter returned before 1626.

Another unmarried woman, who survived the hardships of the first winter, but returned to England and died there, was Humility Cooper. We know almost nothing about her except that she and Henry Sampson were cousins of Edward Tilley and his wife. She is also mentioned as a relative of Richard Clopton, one of the early religious leaders in England.[13]

The "mother" of this group of matrons and maidens, who survived the winters of 1621-2, was undoubtedly Mistress Mary Brewster. Wife of the Elder, she shared his religious faith and

9   Life of Pilgrim Alden; Augustus E. Alden; Boston, 1902.

10   Bradford's History of Plymouth Plantation; Appendix.

11   The England and Holland of the Pilgrims.

12   N. E. Gen. Hist. Reg., 45, 56.

13   N. E. Gen. Hist.; iv, 108.

zeal, and exercised a strong moral influence upon the women and children. Pastor John Robinson, in a letter to Governor Bradford, in 1623, refers to "her weake and decayed state of body," but she lived until April 17, 1627, according to records in "the Brewster Book." She was only fifty-seven years at her death but, as Bradford said with tender appreciation, "her great and continuall labours, with other crosses and sorrows, hastened it before y'e time." As Elder Brewster "could fight as well as he could pray," could build his own house and till his own land,[14] so, we may believe, his wife was efficient in all domestic ways. When her strength failed, it is pleasant to think that she accepted graciously the loving assistance of the younger women to whom she must have seemed, in her presence, like a benediction. Her married life was fruitful; five children lived to maturity and two or more had died in Holland. The Elder was "wise and discreet and well-spoken—of a cheerful spirit, sociable and pleasant among his friends, undervaluing himself and his abilities and sometimes overvaluing others."[15] Such a person is sure to be a delightful companion. To these attractive qualities the Elder added another proof of tact and wisdom: "He always thought it were better for ministers to pray oftener and divide their prayers, than be long and tedious in the same."

While Mistress Brewster did not excel the women of her day, probably, in education, for to read easily and to write were not considered necessary graces for even the better-bred classes,— she could appreciate the thirty-eight copies of the Scriptures which were found among her husband's four hundred volumes; *these* would be familiar to her, but the sixty-four books in Latin would not be read by the women of her day. Fortunately, she did not survive, as did her husband, to endure grief from the deaths of the daughters, Fear and Patience, both of whom died before

14   The Pilgrim Republic; John A. Goodwin.

15   Bradford's History of Plymouth Plantation.

1635; nor yet did she realize the bitterness of feeling between the sons, Jonathan and Love, and their differences of opinion in the settlement of the Elder's estate. [16]

A traditional picture has been given[17] of Captain Peregrine White of Marshfield, "riding a black horse and wearing a coat with buttons the size of a silver dollar, vigorous and of a comely aspect to the last,"[18] paying daily visits to his mother, Mistress Susanna White Winslow. We may imagine this elderly matron, sitting in the Winslow arm-chair, with its mark, "Cheapside, 1614,"[19] perhaps wearing the white silk shoulder-cape with its trimmings of embossed velvet which has been preserved, proud that she was privileged to be the mother of this son, the first child born of white parents in New England, proud that she had been the wife of a Governor and Commissioner of eminence, and also the mother of Josiah Winslow, the first native-born Governor of any North American commonwealth. Hers was a record of which any woman of any century might well be proud![20]

In social position and worldly comforts her life was pre-eminent among the colonists. Although Edward Winslow had renounced some of his English wealth, possibly, when he

16   Records of the Colony of New Plymouth.

17   The Pilgrim Republic; John A. Goodwin;
      foot-note, p.181.

18   Account of his death in Boston News Letter, July 31, 1704.

19   This chair and the cape are now In Pilgrim Hall, Plymouth;
      here also are portraits of Edward Winslow and Josiah Winslow
      and the latter's wife, Penelope.

20   More material may be found in Winslow Memorial; Family
      Record, Holton, N. Y., 1877, and in Ancestral Chronological
      Record of the William White Family, 1607-1895, Concord, 1895.

went to Holland and adopted the trade of printer, he "came into his own" again and was in high favor with English courts and statesmen. His services as agent and commissioner, both for the Plymouth colony and later for Cromwell, must have necessitated long absences from home, while his wife remained at Careswell, the estate at Green Harbor, Marshfield, caring for her younger children, Elizabeth and Josiah Winslow. By family tradition, Mistress Susanna was a woman of graceful, aristocratic bearing and of strong character. Sometimes called Anna, as in her marriage record to William White at Leyden, February 11, 1612,[21] she was the sister of Dr. Samuel Fuller. Two children by her first marriage died in 1615 and 1616; with her boy, Resolved, about five or six years old, she came with her husband on *The Mayflower* and, at the end of the voyage, bore her son, Peregrine White.

The tact, courtesy and practical sagacity of Edward Winslow fitted him for the many demands that were made upon his diplomacy. One of the most amusing stories of his experiences as agent for Plymouth colony has been related by himself[22] when, at the request of the Indians, he visited Massasoit, who was ill, and brought about the recovery of this chief by common sense methods of treatment and by a "savory broth" made from Indian corn, sassafras and strawberry leaves, "strained through his handkerchief." The skill with which Winslow cooked the broth and the "relish" of ducks reflected credit upon the household methods of Mistress Winslow.

After 1646, Edward Winslow did not return to Plymouth for any long sojourn, for Cromwell and his advisers had recognized the worth of such a man as commissioner.[23] In 1655 he was sent

---

21   The Mayflower Descendant, vii, 193.

22   Winslow's Relation.

23   State Papers, Colonial Service, 1574-1660. Winthrop

as one of three commissioners against the Spaniards in the West Indies to attack St. Domingo. Because of lack of supplies and harmony among the troops, the attack was a failure. To atone for this the fleet started towards Jamaica, but on the way, near Hispaniola, Winslow was taken ill of fever and died, May 8, 1655; he was buried at sea with a military salute from forty-two guns. The salary paid to Winslow during these years was £1000, which was large for those times. On April 18, 1656, a "representation" from his widow, Susanna, and son was presented to the Lord Protector and council, asking that, although Winslow's death occurred the previous May, the remaining £500 of his year's salary might be paid to satisfy his creditors.

To his wife and family Winslow, doubtless, wrote letters as graceful and interesting as are the few business epistles that are preserved in the Winthrop Papers.[24] That he was anxious, to return to his family is evident from a letter by President Steele of the Society for Propagating the Gospel in New England (in 1650), which Winslow was also serving;[25] "Winslow was unwilling to be longer kept from his family, but his great acquaintance and influence were of service to the cause so great that it was hoped he would remain for a time longer." In his will, which is now in Somerset House, London, dated 1654, he left his estate at Marshfield to his son, Josiah, with the stipulation that his wife, Susanna, should be allowed a full third part thereof through her life.[26] She lived twenty-five years longer, dying in October, 1680, at the estate, Careswell. It is supposed that she was buried on the hillside cemetery of the Daniel Webster estate

Papers, ii, 283.

24   Hutchinson Collections, 110, 153, etc.

25   The Pilgrim Republic; Goodwin, 444.

26   The Mayflower Descendant, iv. i.

in Marshfield, where, amid tangles and flowers, may be located the grave-stones of her children and grandchildren. Sharing with Mistress Susanna White Winslow the distinction of being mother of a child born on *The Mayflower* was Mistress Elizabeth Hopkins, whose son, Oceanus, was named for his birthplace. She was the second wife of Stephen Hopkins, who was one of the leaders with Winslow and Standish on early expeditions. With her stepchildren, Constance and Giles, and her little daughter, Damaris, she bore the rigors of those first years, bore other children,—Caleb, Ruth, Deborah and Elizabeth,—and cared for a large estate, including servants and many cattle. The inventory of the Hopkins estate revealed an abundance of beds and bedding, yellow and green rugs, curtains and spinning-wheels, and much wearing apparel. The home-life surely had incidents of excitement, as is shown by the accusations and fines against Stephen Hopkins for "suffering excessive drinking at his house, 1637, when William Reynolds was drunk and lay under the table," and again for "suffering men to drink in his house on the Lord's Day, both before and after the meeting—and allowing his servant and others to drink more than for ordinary refreshing and to play shovell board and such like misdemeanors."[27] Such lapses in conduct at the Hopkins house were atoned for by the services which Stephen Hopkins rendered to the colony as explorer, assistant to the governor and other offices which suited his reliable and fearless disposition.

These occasional "misdemeanors" in the Hopkins household were slight compared with the records against "the black sheep" of the colony, the family of Billingtons from London. The mother, Helen or Ellen, did not seem to redeem the reputation of husband and sons; traditionally she was called "the scold." After her husband had been executed in 1630, for the first murder in the colony, for he had waylaid and killed John Newcomen, she married Gregory Armstrong. She had various controversies

27   Records of the Colony of New Plymouth.

in court with her son and others. In 1636, she was accused of slander by "Deacon" John Doane,—she had charged him with unfairness in mowing her pasture lot,—and she was sentenced to a fine of five pounds and "to sit in the stocks and be publickly whipt."[28] Her second husband died in 1650 and she lived several years longer, occupying a "tenement" granted to her in her son's house at North Plymouth. Apparently her son, John, after his fractious youth, died; Francis married Christian Penn, the widow of Francis Eaton.

Their children seem to have "been bound out" for service while the parents were convicted of trying to entice the children away from their work and, consequently, they were punished by sitting in the stocks on "lecture days."[29] In his later life, Francis Billington became more stable in character and served on committees. His last offense was the mild one "of drinking tobacco on the high-way." Apparently, Helen Billington had many troubles and little sympathy in the Plymouth colony.

As companions to these matrons of the pioneer days were four maidens who must have been valuable as assistants in housework and care of the children,—Priscilla Mullins, Mary Chilton, Elizabeth Tilley and Constance Hopkins. The first three had been orphaned during that first winter; probably, they became members of the households of Elder Brewster and Governor Carver. All have left names that are most honorably cherished by their many descendants. Priscilla Mullins has been celebrated in romance and poetry. Very little real knowledge exists about her and many of the surmises would be more interesting if they could be proved. She was well-born, for her father, at his death, was mentioned with regret [30] as "a man pious and well-

---

28   Records of the Colony of New Plymouth.

29   The Pilgrim Republic; Goodwin.

30   New England Memorial; Morton.

deserving, endowed also with considerable outward estate; and had it been the will of God, that he had survived, might have proved an useful instrument in his place." There was a family tradition of a castle, Molyneux or Molines, in Normandy. The title of *Mr.* indicated that he was a man of standing and he was a counsellor in state and church. Perhaps he died on shipboard at Plymouth, because his, will, dated April 2, 1621, was witnessed by John Carver, Christopher Jones and Giles Heald, probably the captain and surgeon of the ship, *Mayflower.*

This will, which has been recently found in Dorking, Surrey, England, has had important influence upon research. We learn that an older sister, Sarah Blunden, living in Surrey, was named as administratrix, and that a son, William (who came to Plymouth before 1637) was to have money, bonds and stocks in England. Goods in Virginia and more money,—ten pounds each,—were bequeathed equally to his wife Alice, his daughter Priscilla and the younger son, Joseph. Interesting also is the item of "xxj dozen shoes and thirteene paire of boots wch I give unto the Companie's hands for forty pounds at seaven yeares." If the Company would not accept the rate, these shoes and boots were to be for the equal benefit of his wife and son, William. To his friend, John Carver, he commits his wife and children and also asks for a "special eye to my man Robert wch hath not so approved himself as I would he should have done."[31] Before this will was probated, July 23, 1621, John Carver, Mistress Alice Mullins, the son, Joseph, and the man, Robert Carter (or Cartier) were all dead, leaving Priscilla to carry on the work to which they had pledged their lives. Perhaps, the brother and sister in England were children of an earlier marriage,[32] as Alice Mullins has been spoken of as a second wife.

Priscilla was about twenty years old when she came to

---

31   Pilgrim Alden, by Augustus E. Alden, Boston, 1902.

32   Gen. Hist. Register, 40; 62-3.

Plymouth. By tradition she was handsome, witty, deft and skilful as spinner and cook. Into her life came John Alden, a cooper of unknown family, who joined the Pilgrims at Southampton, under promise to stay a year. Probably he was not the first suitor for Priscilla's hand, for tradition affirmed that she had been sought in Leyden. The single sentence by Bradford tells the story of their romance: "being a hop[e]full yong man was much desired, but left to his owne liking to go or stay when he came here; but he stayed, and maryed here." With him he brought a Bible, printed 1620,[33] probably a farewell gift or purchase as he left England. When the grant of land and cattle was made in 1627, he was twenty-eight years old, and had in his family, Priscilla, his wife, a daughter, Elizabeth, aged three, and a son, John, aged one.[34]

The poet, Longfellow, was a descendant of Priscilla Alden, and he had often heard the story of the courtship of Priscilla by Miles Standish, through John Alden as his proxy. It was said to date back to a poem, "Courtship," by Moses Mullins, 1672. In detail it was given by Timothy Alden in "American Epitaphs," 1814,[35] but there are here some deflections from facts as later research has revealed them. The magic words of romance, "Why don't you speak for yourself, John?" are found in this early narrative.

There was more than romance in the lives of John and Priscilla Alden as the "vital facts" indicate. Their first home was at Town Square, Plymouth, on the site of the first schoolhouse but, by 1633, they lived upon a farm of one hundred and sixty-nine acres in Duxbury. Their first house here was about three hundred feet from the present Alden house, which was

---

33   Now in Pilgrim Hall, Plymouth.

34   Records of the Colony of New Plymouth.

35   American Epitaphs, 1814; iii, 139.

built by the son, Jonathan, and is now occupied by the eighth John Alden. It must have been a lonely farmstead for Priscilla, although she made rare visits, doubtless on an ox or a mare, or in an ox-cart with her children, to see Barbara Standish at Captain's Hill, or to the home of Jonathan Brewster, a few miles distant. As farmer, John Alden was not so successful as he would have been at his trade of cooper. Moreover, he gave much of his time to the service of the colony throughout his manhood, acting as assistant to the Governor, treasurer, surveyor, agent and military recruit. Like many another public servant of his day and later, he "became low in his estate" and was allowed a small gratuity of ten pounds because "he hath been occationed to spend time at the Courts on the Countryes occasion and soe hath done this many yeares."[36] He had also been one of the eight "undertakers" who, in 1627, assumed the debts and financial support of the Plymouth colony.

Eleven children had been born to John and Priscilla Alden, five sons and six daughters. Sarah married Alexander Standish and so cemented the two families in blood as well as in friendship. Ruth, who married John Bass, became the ancestress of John Adams and John Quincy Adams. Elizabeth, who married William Pabodie, had thirteen children, eleven of them girls, and lived to be ninety-three years; at her death the *Boston News Letter* [37] extolled her as "exemplary, virtuous and pious and her memory is blessed." Possibly with all her piety she had a good share of the independence of spirit which was accredited to her mother; in her husband's will[38] she is given her "third at Little Compton" and an abundance of household stuff, but with this reservation,—"If she will not be contented with her thirds at

36 Records of the Colony of New Plymouth.

37 June 17, 1717.

38 The Mayflower Descendant, vi, 129.

Little Compton, but shall claim her thirds in both Compton and Duxbury or marry again, I do hereby make voyde all my bequest unto her and she shall share only the parte as if her husband died intestate." A portrait of her shows dress of rich materials.

Captain John Alden seems to have been more adventuresome than the other boys in Priscilla's family. He was master of a merchantman in Boston and commander of armed vessels which supplied marine posts with provisions. Like his sister, Elizabeth, he had thirteen children. He was once accused of witchcraft, when he was present at a trial, and was imprisoned fifteen weeks without being allowed bail.[39] He escaped and hurried to Duxbury, where he must have astonished his mother by the recital of his adventures. He left an estate of £2059, in his will, two houses, one of wood worth four hundred pounds, and another of brick worth two hundred and seventy pounds, besides much plate, brass and money and debts amounting to £1259, "the most of which are desperite." A tablet in the wall of the Old South Church at Copley Square, Boston, records his death at the age of seventy-five, March, 1701. He was an original member of this church. Perhaps Priscilla varied her peaceful life by visits to this affluent son in Boston. There is no evidence of the date of Priscilla Alden's death or the place of her burial. She was living and present, with her husband, at Josiah Winslow's funeral in 1680. She must have died before her husband, for in his Inventory, 1686, he makes no mention of her. He left a small estate of only a little over forty pounds, although he had given to his sons land in Duxbury, Taunton, Middleboro and Bridgewater.[40] Probably Priscilla also bestowed some of her treasures upon her children before she died. Some of her spoons, pewter and candle-sticks have been traced by

39   History of Witchcraft; Upham.

40   The Mayflower Descendant, iii, 10. The Story of a Pilgrim
       Family; Rev. John Alden; Boston, 1890.

inheritance. It is not likely that she was "rich in this world's goods" through her marriage, but she had a husband whose fidelity to state and religion have ever been respected. To his memory Rev. John Cotton wrote some elegiac verses; Justin Winsor has emphasized the honor which is still paid to the name of John Alden in Duxbury and Plymouth:[41] "He was possessed of a sound judgment and of talents which, though not brilliant, were by no means ordinary—decided, ardent, resolute, and persevering, indifferent to danger, a bold and hardy man, stern, austere and unyielding and of incorruptible integrity." The name of Mary Chilton is pleasant to the ear and imagination. Chilton Street and Chiltonville in Plymouth, and the Chilton Club in Boston, keep alive memories of this girl who was, by persistent tradition, the first woman who stepped upon the rock of landing at Plymouth harbor. This tradition was given in writing, in 1773, by Ann Taylor, the grandchild of Mary Chilton and John Winslow.[42] Her father, James Chilton, sometimes with the Dutch spelling, Tgiltron, was a man of influence among the early leaders, but he died at Cape Cod, December 8, 1620. He came from Canterbury, England, to Holland. By the records on the Roll of Freemen of the City of Canterbury,[43] he is named as James Chylton, tailor, "Freeman by Gift, 1583." Earlier Chiltons,—William, spicer, and Nicholas, clerk,—are classified as "Freemen by Redemption." Three children were baptized in St. Paul's Church, Canterbury,—Isabella, 1586; Jane, 1589; and Ingle, 1599. Isabella was married in Leyden to Roger Chandler five years before *The Mayflower* sailed. Evidently, Mary bore the same name as an older sister whose burial is recorded at St.

---

41   History of Duxbury; Winsor.

42   History of Plymouth; James Thatcher.

43   Probably this freedom was given, by the city or some board therein, as mark of respect. N. E. Gen. Hist. Reg., 63, 201.

Martin's, Canterbury, in 1593. Isaac Chilton, a glass-maker, may have been brother or cousin of James. Of Mary's mother almost nothing has been found except mention of her death during the infection of 1621.[44]

When *The Fortune* arrived in November, 1621, it brought Mary Chilton's future husband among the passengers,—John Winslow, younger brother of Edward. Not later than 1627 they were married and lived at first in the central settlement, and later in Plain Dealing, North Plymouth. They had ten children. The son, John, was Brigadier-General in the Army. John Winslow, Sr., seemed to show a spirit of enterprise by the exchange and sale of his "lots" in Plymouth and afterwards in Boston where he moved his family, and became a successful owner and master of merchant ships. Here he acquired land on Devonshire Street and Spring Lane and also on Marshall Lane and Hanover Street. From Plans and Deeds, prepared by Annie Haven Thwing,[45] one may locate a home of Mary Chilton Winslow in Boston, a lot 72 and 85, 55 and 88, in the rear of the first Old South Church, at the southwest corner of Joyliffe's Lane, now Devonshire Street, and Spring Lane. It was adjacent to land owned by John Winthrop and Richard Parker. By John Winslow's will, probated May 21, 1674, he bequeathed this house, land, gardens and a goodly sum of money and shares of stock to his wife and children. The house and stable, with land, was inventoried for £490 and the entire estate for £2946-14-10. He had a Katch *Speedwell*, with cargoes of pork, sugar and tobacco, and a Barke *Mary*, whose produce was worth £209; these were to be divided among his children. His money was also to be divided, including 133 "peeces of eight."[46]

44   Bradford's History of Plymouth Plantation; Appendix.

45   Massachusetts Historical Society, Boston. Also dimensions in Bowditch Title Books: 26: 315.

46   The Mayflower Descendant, 111, 129 (1901).

Interesting as are the items of this will, which afford proofs that Mary Chilton as matron had luxuries undreamed of in the days of 1621, *her* will is even more important for us. It is one of the three *original* known wills of *Mayflower* passengers, the others being those of Edward Winslow and Peregrine White. Mary Chilton's will is in the Suffolk Registry of Probate,[47] Boston, in good condition, on paper 18 by 14 inches. The will was made July 31, 1676. Among other interesting bequests are: to my daughter Sarah (Middlecot) "my Best gowne and Pettecoat and my silver beare bowl" and to each of her children "a silver cup with a handle." To her grandchild, William Payne, was left her "great silver Tankard" and to her granddaughter, Ann Gray, "a trunk of Linning" (linen) with bed, bolsters and ten pounds in money. Many silver spoons and "ruggs" were to be divided. To her grandchild, Susanna Latham, was definite allotment of "Petty coate with silke Lace." In the inventory one may find commentary upon the valuation of these goods—"silk gowns and pettecoats" for £6-10, twenty-two napkins at seven shillings, and three "great pewter dishes" and twenty small pieces of pewter for two pounds, six shillings. She had gowns, mantles, head bands, fourteen in number, seventeen linen caps, six white aprons, pocket-handkerchiefs and all other articles of dress. Mary Chilton Winslow could not write her name, but she made a very neat mark, M. She was buried beneath the Winslow coat of arms at the front of King's Chapel Burial-ground in Boston. She closely rivalled, if she did not surpass in wealth and social position, her sister-in-law, Susanna White Winslow.

Elizabeth Tilley had a more quiet life, but she excelled her associates among these girls of Plymouth in one way,—she could write her name very well. Possibly she was taught by her husband, John Howland who left, in his inventory, an inkhorn, and who wrote records and letters often for the colonists. For many years, until the discovery and printing of Bradford's

47   This will Is reprinted In The Mayflower Descendant, I: 85.

History of Plymouth Plantation in 1856, it was assumed that Elizabeth Tilley was either the daughter or granddaughter of Governor Carver; such misstatement even appears upon the Howland tombstone in the old burying-ground at Plymouth. Efforts to explain by assuming a second marriage of Carver or a first marriage of Howland fail to convince, for, surely, such relationships would have been mentioned by Bradford, Winslow, Morton or Prence. After the death of her parents, during the first winter, Elizabeth remained with the Carver household until that was broken by death; afterwards she was included in the family over which John Howland was considered "head"; according to the grant of 1624 he was given an acre each for himself, Elizabeth Tilley, Desire Minter, and the boy, William Latham.

The step-mother of Elizabeth Tilley bore a Dutch name, Bridget Van De Veldt.[48] Elizabeth was ten or twelve years younger than her husband, at least, for he was twenty-eight years old in 1620. They were married, probably, by 1623-4, for the second child, John, was born in 1626. It is not known how long Howland had been with the Pilgrims at Leyden; he may have come there with Cushman in 1620 or, possibly, he joined the company at Southampton. His ancestry is still in some doubt in spite of the efforts to trace it to one John Howland, "gentleman and citizen and salter" of London.[49] Probably the outfit necessary for the voyage was furnished to him by Carver, and the debt was to be paid in some service, clerical or other; in no other sense was he a "servant." He signed the compact of *The Mayflower* and was one of the "ten principal men" chosen to select a site for the colony. For many years he was prominent in civic affairs of the state and church. He was among the liberals towards Quakers as were his brothers who came later to Marshfield,—Arthur and

48   N. E. Gen. Hist. Reg., i, 34.

49   Recollections of John Howland, etc. E. H. Stone,
         Providence, 1857.

Henry. At Rocky Neck, near the Jones River in Kingston, as it is now called, the Howland household was prosperous, with nine children to keep Elizabeth Tilley's hands occupied. She lived until past eighty years, and died at the home of her daughter, Lydia Howland Brown, in Swanzey, in 1687. Among the articles mentioned in her will are many books of religious type. Her husband's estate as inventoried was not large, but mentioned such useful articles as silk neckcloths, four dozen buttons and many skeins of silk.[50]

Constance or Constanta Hopkins was probably about the same age as Elizabeth Tilley, for she was married before 1627 to Nicholas Snow, who came in *The Ann*. They had twelve children, and among the names one recognizes such familiar patronymics of the two families as Mark, Stephen, Ruth and Elizabeth. Family tradition has ascribed beauty and patience to this maiden who, doubtless, served well both in her father's large family and in the community. Her step-sister, Damaris, married Jacob Cooke, son of the Pilgrim, Francis Cooke.

A CHAPTER FROM
The Women Who Came in the Mayflower, 1920

---

50   The Mayflower Descendant, ii, 70.

AN EXCERPT
OF LETTER X

By Fredrika Bremer

BOSTON,
February 1st.

Most hearty thanks my dear little heart for your letter of the 15th of December: it is so inexpressibly dear to me to hear and see how things are at home, as well in the little as the great. If you only had not your usual winter complaint. Ah that winter! but I am glad nevertheless that you feel a little better in December than in November, and assure myself that in January you will be better still. And then comes the prospect of summer and the baths of Marstrand. Mamma writes that you were evidently stronger for your summer visit to Marstrand. And you will be yet stronger still after your next summer's visit. But your ideal— that farm-yard servant-girl, who took the bull by the horns, when will you come up to that?

My strength has increased considerably for some time, thanks to my excellent Dr. Osgood and his little nothing-powders and globules. And when I feel myself well my soul is cheerful and well, and then my mind is, full of thoughts which make me happy; then I am glad to be on the Pilgrims' soil; that soil which the Pilgrim-fathers as they are here called, first trod, first consecrated as the home of religious and civil liberty, and from winch little band the intellectual cultivation of this part of the world proceeds and has proceeded.

It was in the month of December, 1620, when the little ship, the "Mayflower," anchored on the shore of Massachussets, with the first Pilgrims, one hundred in number. They were of that party which in England was called Puritan; which had arisen after the Reformation, and in consequence of it, and which required a more perfect Reformation than that which Luther had brought about. But they desired more; to give full activity to the truth which Luther promulgated when he asserted man's direct relationship to God through Jesus Christ, denying any right of the Church or of tradition to interfere in the determination of that which should be believed or taught, and demanding liberty for every human being to examine and judge for himself in matters of faith, acknowledging no other law or authority than God's Word in the Bible. The Puritans demanded on these grounds their right to reject the old ceremonial of the Established Church, and in the place of those empty forms, the right to choose their own minister; the right to worship God in spirit and in truth, and the right of deciding for themselves their form of Church government. Puritanism was the rising of that old divine leaven which Christ had foretold should one day "leaven the whole lump" of the spiritual life of liberty in Jesus Christ. The charter of freedom given by him was the watchword of the Puritans. With this in their hand and on their lips they dared to enter into combat with the dominant Episcopal Church; refused to unite themselves with it, called themselves non-conformists, and held separate assemblies or religious conventicles. The State Church and the government rose in opposition and passed an act against conventicles.

But the Puritans and the conventicles increased year by year in England. Noble priests, such as Wicliff, and many of the respectable of the land, became their adherents. Queen Elizabeth treated them however with caution and respect. Her successor, King James, raved blindly against them, saying,—"I will make them conform, or I will harry them out of the land; or worse, only hang them; that is all!" And the choice was given them; either to return to the State Church, or imprisonment and death. This only strengthened the opposition; "For," says Thomas Carlyle, otherwise tolerably bitter in his criticism on human nature, "people do human nature an injustice when they believe that the instigation to great actions is self-interest, worldly profit or pleasure. No, that which instigates to great undertakings, and produces great things, is the prospect of conflict, persecution, suffering, martyrdom, for the truth's sake."

In one of the northern counties of England, a little company of men and women, inhabitants of small towns and villages, united in the resolve to risk all for the open acknowledgment of their pure faith, conformably with the teachings of which they determined to live. They were people of the lowest condition, principally artisans or tillers of the soil; men who lived by the hard labour of their hands, and who were accustomed to combat with the severe circumstances of life. Holland at this time offered to them, as it did to all the oppressed combatants for the truth, a place of refuge; and to Holland the little knot of Puritans resolved to flee. They escaped from their vigilant persecutors through great dangers, and Leyden in Holland became their city of refuge. But they did not prosper there; they felt that it was not the place for them; they knew that they were to be pilgrims on the earth seeking a father-land: and amid their struggles with the hard circumstances of daily life, the belief existed in their souls that they were called upon to accomplish a higher work for humanity than that which consisted with their present lot. "They felt themselves moved by zeal and by hope to make known the Gospel and extend the kingdom of Christ in the far-distant land of the New World; yes, if they even should be merely as stepping-stones for others to carry forth so great a work."

They asked, and after great difficulty obtained, the consent of the English government to emigrate to North America, where they might endeavour to labour for the glory of God and the advantage of England.

They chartered two ships, the "Mayflower" and "Speedwell," to bear them across the sea. Only the youngest and strongest of the little band, who voluntarily offered themselves, were selected to go out first on the perilous voyage; and that after they had publicly prepared themselves by fasting and prayer. "Let us," said they, "beseech of God to open a right way for us and our little ones, and for all our substance!"

Only a portion of those who had gone out to Holland found room in the two vessels. Among those who remained was also their noble teacher and leader, John Robinson. But from the shores of the Old World he uttered, as a parting address, these glorious words—"I charge you, before God and his blessed angels, that you follow me no farther than you have seen me follow the Lord Jesus Christ. The Lord has yet more truth to break forth out of his Holy Word. I cannot sufficiently bewail the condition of the reformed churches who are come to a period in religion, and will go no farther at present than the instruments of their reformation. Luther and Calvin were great and shining lights in their times, yet they penetrated not into the whole counsel of God. I beseech you remember it—'tis an article of your Church covenant—that you be ready to receive whatever truth shall be made known to you from the written Word of God."

"When our vessels were ready to receive us on board," writes one of the party, "the brethren who had fasted and prayed with us gave us a parting feast at the house of our minister, which was roomy; and then, after shedding many tears, we refreshed ourselves with the singing of hymns, making joyful music in our hearts as well as with our voices, for many of our community were very skilful in music. After this they accompanied us to Dreft Harbour, where we were to go on board, and there we were entertained anew. And after our minister had prayed with us, and floods of tears had been shed, they accompanied us on board. But we were in no condition to talk one with another of the exceeding great grief of parting. From our vessel, however, we gave them a salutation; and then extending our hands to each other, and lifting up our hearts for each other to the Lord our God, and so set sail."

A prosperous wind quickly conveyed the Pilgrims to the English shore; and then the smallest of the vessels, the "Speedwell," was compelled to lie-to for repairs. But scarcely had they again left the English coast with sails unfurled for the Atlantic, when the captain of the "Speedwell" and his company lost courage in the prospect of the greatness of the undertaking and all its perils, and desired to return to England. The people of the "Mayflower" agreed that "it was very grievous and discouraging." And now the little band of resolute men and women, several of the latter far advanced in pregnancy, persevered in their undertaking, and with their children and their household stuff, an entire floating village, they sailed onward in the "Mayflower" across the great sea towards the New World, and at the most rigorous season of the year. After a stormy voyage of sixty-three days, the Pilgrims beheld the shores of the New World, and in two more days the "Mayflower" cast anchor in the harbour of Cape Cod, on the coast of Massachussets.

Yet, before they land, and whilst the "Mayflower" yet rests upon the waves of the deep, they assemble to deliberate on some constituted form of government; and, drawing up the following compact, they formed themselves into a voluntary body-politic.

"In the name of God, Amen. We, whose names are underwritten, the loyal subjects of our dread sovereign King James, having undertaken, for the glory of God and advancement of the Christian faith, and honour of our king and country, a voyage to plant the first colony in the northern parts of Virginia, do, by these presents, solemnly and mutually, in the presence of God and one of another, covenant and combine ourselves together into a civil body-politic, for our better ordering and preservation, and furtherance of the ends aforesaid; and by virtue hereof, to enact, constitute, and frame such just and equal laws, ordinances, acts, constitutions, and offices, from time to time, as shall be thought most convenient for the general good of the colony. Unto which we promise all due submission and obedience."

This instrument was signed by all the men in company, forty-one in number. Thus was framed, in the cabin of the "Mayflower," the most truly democratic constitution which the world had yet seen. That democratic, self-governing community came forth in a state of complete organisation from the "Mayflower" to the shore of the New World.

Like Abraham, the pilgrim-band went forth, obedient to the voice of God, into a land to them unknown, and not themselves fully cognisant of the work they were called to do.

They went forth to seek a free virgin soil on which to found their pure church, for the glory of God's kingdom, and unconsciously to themselves, likewise, to found, in so doing, a new civil community which should be a home and a community for all people of the earth. The "Mayflower" gave birth to popular constitutional liberty at the same time that it established the pure vitality of religion: and that was but natural, the latter included the former. The Pilgrims conveyed with them the new life of the New World without being themselves conscious of it.

They landed on a rock, since called "Plymouth Rock," or, also, "The Pilgrims' Rock." It was a young girl who was first permitted to spring from the boat on shore. It was her light foot which first touched the rock. It was at the commencement of winter when the pilgrims reached the new land; and they were met by cold, and storm, and adverse circumstances. They made an excursion of discovery inland, and found, in one place, a little corn, but no habitations, only Indian graves.

They had been but a few days on shore, and were beginning to build habitations as a defence against the storms and the snow, when the Sunday occurred, and it is characteristic of that first Puritan community that, under their circumstances, they rested from all labour, and kept the Sabbath uninterruptedly and with all solemnity.

I have lately read a narrative, or, more properly speaking, a chronicle, kept as a diary of the life of the first colonists, their wars and labours during the first year of their settlement. It is a simple chronicle, without any wordiness or parade, without any attempt at making it romantic or beautiful, but which affected me more, and went more directly to the depths of the heart, than many a touching novel; and which seemed to me grander than many a heroic poem. For how great in all its unpretendingness was this life, this labour! What courage, what perseverance, what steadfastness, what unwavering trust in that little band! How they aided one another, these men and women; how they persevered though all sorrow and adversity, in life and in death. They lived surrounded by dangers, in warfare with the natives; they suffered from climate, from the want of habitations and conveniences, from the want of food; they lay sick; they saw their beloved die; they suffered hunger and cold; but still they persevered. They saw the habitations they had built destroyed, and they built afresh. Amid their struggles with want and adversity, amid the Indian's rain of arrows, they founded their commonwealth and their church; they formed laws, established schools, and all that could give stability and strength to a human community. They wielded the sword with one hand and guided the plough with the other. Amid increasing jeopardy of life, they in particular reflected on the welfare of their successors, and framed laws which every one must admire for their sagacity, purity, and humanity. Even the animal creation was placed under the protection of these laws, and punishment ordained for the mistreatment of the beast.

During the first year their sufferings and hardships were extreme. "I have seen men," writes an eye-witness, "stagger by reason of faintness for want of food."

The harvest of the third year was abundant, and now, instead of, as hitherto, each one labouring for the common benefit, each colonist worked alone for his own family and his own advantage. This gave an impulse to labour and to good management. And when they had lived through the time of want, a time of prosperity commenced, and the colony increased rapidly in power and extent. In a few years it was said of it "that you might live there from one year's end to another without seeing a drunkard, hearing an oath, or meeting with a beggar." They who survived the first period of suffering lived to be extremely old.

It is not to be wondered at, that from a parentage strong as this, should be derived a race destined to become a great people. Other colonies more to the south, whose morals were more lax, and whose purpose of life was of a lower range, had either died out or maintained merely a feeble existence amid warfare with the natives, suffering from the climate and encompassed with difficulties. The Puritans, on the contrary, with their lofty aims of life, their steadfast faith and pure manners, became the conquerors of the desert and the lawgivers of the New World. Nor do I know of any nation which ever had a nobler foundation or nobler founders. The whole of humanity had taken a step onward with the Pilgrim-fathers in the New World. The work which they had to do concerned the whole human race.

And when from the land of the Pilgrims I look abroad over the United States, I see everywhere, in the south as well as the north and the west, the country populated, the empire founded by a people composed of all peoples, who suffered persecution for their faith, who sought freedom of conscience and peace on a new free soil. I see the Huguenot and the Herrnhutter in the south, and along the Mississippi, in the west, Protestants and Catholics, who, from all the countries of Europe seek for and find there those most precious treasures of mankind; and who in that affluent soil establish flourishing communities under the social and free laws instituted by the oldest Pilgrims.

To them belongs the honour of that new creation, and from them even to this day, proceed the creative ideas in the social life of the New World; and whether willingly or unwillingly, widely differing people and religious sects have received the impression of their spirit. Domestic manners, social intercourse, form themselves by it; the life and church-government of all religious bodies recognise the influence of the Puritan standard,

"Live conformably to conscience; let thy whole behaviour bear witness to thy religious confession." And that form of government which was organised by the little community of the "Mayflower," has become the vital principle in all the United States of America, and is the same which now on the coast of the Pacific Ocean controls and directs with quiet power the wild free spirits of California, educating them to self-government and obedience to law.

The old colonies have sent out to all parts of the Union crowds of pilgrims, sons and daughters, and they constitute at this time more than one-third of the population of the United States of North America. They were nevertheless most numerous in the north, and there they have left the strongest impression of their spirit.

When I contemplate that Puritan community as it exists in our time, about two centuries after its first establishment, it seems to me that there are two main springs within its impulsive heart; the one is a tendency towards the ideal of moral life, the other impels it to conquer the earth, that is to say, the material power and products of life. The men of the New World, and pre-eminently the men of New England, (humourously called Yankees) have a passion for acquisition, and for this object think nothing of labour—even the hardest—and nothing of trouble; nay, to travel half over the world to do a good stroke of business, is a very little thing. The Viking element in the Yankee's nature, and which he perhaps originally inherited from the Scandinavian Vikings, compels him incessantly to work, to undertake, to accomplish something which tends either to his own improvement or that of others. For when he has improved himself, he thinks, if not before, of employing his pound for the public good. He gets money, but only to spend. He puts it by, but not for selfish purposes. Public spirit is the animating principle of his life, and he prefers to leave behind him the name of an esteemed and beloved citizen rather than a large property. He likes to leave that which he has acquired to some institution or benevolent establishment, which thenceforth commonly bears his name. And I know those whose benevolence is so pure that they slight even this reward.

The moral ideal of man and of society seems to be clearly understood here, and all the more clearly in those northern states which have derived their population from the old colonies. From conversation with sensible idealists among my friends as well as from the attention I have given to the spirit of public life here, I have acquainted myself with the demands made by man and by society, and for which young America combats as for its true purpose and mission, and they appear to be as follows:—

Every human being must be strictly true to his own individuality; must stand alone with God, and from this innermost point of view must act alone conformably to his own consciencious convictions.

There is no virtue peculiar to the one sex which is not also a virtue in the other. Man must in morals and conduct come up to the purity of woman.

Woman must possess the means of the highest development of which her nature is capable. She must equally with man have the opportunity of cultivating and developing her intellect. She must possess the same rights in her endeavours after freedom and happiness as man.

The honour of labour and the rewards of labour ought to be equal to all. All labour is in itself honourable, and must be regarded as such. Every honest labourer must be honoured.

The principle of equality must govern in society.

Man must become just and good through a just and good mode of treatment. Good must call forth good.

(This reminds me of that beautiful Swedish legend of the middle ages, about the youth who was changed by a witch into a wehr-wolf, but who, at the sound of his Christian name, spoken by a loving voice, would recover his original shape.)

The community must give to every one of its members the best possible chance of developing his human abilities, so that he may come into possession of his human rights. This must be done in part by legislation, which must remove all hindrances and impediments; in part by public educational institutions which shall give to all alike the opportunity of the full development of the human faculties, until they reach the age when they may be considered as capable of caring for and determining for themselves.

The ideal of society is attained in part by the individual coming up to his own ideal; in part by those free institutions and associations in which mankind is brought into a brotherly relation with each other, and by mutual responsibility.

Everything for all is the true object of society. Every one must be able to enjoy all the good things of earth, as well temporal as spiritual; every one according to his own capacity of enjoyment. None must be excluded who does not exclude himself. The chance of regaining his place in society must be given to everyone. For this cause the prison must be an institution for improvement, a second school for those who need it. Society must in its many-sided development, so organise itself that all may be able to attain everything: Everything for all.

The ideal of the man of America seems to me to be, purity of intention, decision in will, energy in action, simplicity and gentleness in manner and demeanour. Hence it is that there is a something tender and chivalric in his behaviour to woman, which is infinitely becoming to him. In every woman he respects his own mother.

In the same way it appeared to me that the ideal of the woman of America, of the woman of the New World, is, independence in character, gentleness of demeanour and manner.

The American's ideal of happiness seems to me to be, marriage and home, combined with public activity. To have a wife, his own house and home, his own little piece of land; to take care of these, and to beautify them, at the same time doing some good to the state or to the city—this seems to me to be the object of human life with most men; a journey to Europe to see perfected cities, and—ruins belong to it, as a desirable episode.

Of the American home I have seen enough, and heard enough, for me to be able to say that the women have in general all the rule there which they wish to have. Woman is the centre and the lawgiver in the home of the New World, and the American man loves that it should be so. He wishes that his wife should have her own will at home, and he loves to obey it. In proof of this, I have heard the words of a young man quoted; "I hope that my wife will have her own will in the house, and if she has not I'll make her have it!" I must, however, say, that in the happy homes in which I lived I saw the wife equally careful to guide herself by the wishes of her husband as he was to indulge hers. Affection and sound reason make all things equal.

The educational institutions for woman are in general much superior to those of Europe; and perhaps the most important work which America is doing for the future of humanity, consists in her treatment and education of woman. Woman's increasing value as a teacher, and the employment of her as such in public schools, even in those for boys, is a public fact in these states which greatly delights me. Seminaries have been established to educate her for this vocation (I hope to be able to visit that at West Newton, in the neighbourhood of Boston, and which was originated by Horace Mann). It even seems as if the daughters of New England had a peculiar faculty and love for this employment. Young girls of fortune devote themselves to it. The daughters of poor farmers go to work in the manufactories a sufficient time to earn the necessary sum to put themselves to school, and thus to become teachers in due course. Whole crowds of school-teachers go hence to the western and southern states, where schools are daily being established, and placed under their direction. The young daughters of New England are universally commended for their character and ability. Even Waldo Emerson, who does not easily praise, spoke in commendation of them. They learn in the schools the classics, mathematics, physics, algebra, with great ease, and pass their examinations like young men. Not long since a young lady in Nantucket, not far from Boston, distinguished herself in astronomy, discovered a new planet, and received, in consequence, a medal from the King of Prussia. . .

AN EXCERPT FROM
The Homes of the New World, 1853

Made in United States
Orlando, FL
18 November 2023

39159284R00079